War C

War Child

A Story of Survival

JULIET LAC

MAINSTREAM
PUBLISHING
EDINBURGH AND LONDON

First published in Great Britain in 2008 by
MAINSTREAM PUBLISHING COMPANY (EDINBURGH) LTD
7 Albany Street
Edinburgh EH1 3UG

ISBN 9781845962821

This book is a work of non-fiction based on the life, experiences and
recollections of the author. In some cases, names of people, places,
dates, sequences or the detail of events have been changed to protect
the privacy of others. The author has stated to the publishers that,
except in such respects, not affecting the substantial accuracy
of the work, the contents of this book are true.

A catalogue record for this book is available
from the British Library

Typeset in Present and Sabon

Printed in Great Britain by
William Clowes Ltd, Beccles, Suffolk

I would like to dedicate this book to the most important people in my life: my mother, Suong; my sons, Kenny and Sonny; and my friends, Sara and Marina

Acknowledgements

From the start, I wanted to write this book myself, but I knew that I was not a professional writer. I am indebted to Vernita Irvin for her friendship and guidance, as without her I would never have had the courage to write it.

I owe a lot to my son, Kenny, who was the reason I wanted to tell my story. I appreciate Carol Strobel's efforts, which have encouraged me to reveal my life and survival on three continents to the people around the world. I am grateful to the team at Mainstream Publishing for helping me in making my dream come true.

Necessarily, some names have been omitted, but they are not forgotten – they are in my heart and mind. My deepest thanks to everyone!

Contents

The Legend of Thuy Tinh

Long ago in Vietnam, there was a great ruler named Emperor Hung Vuong the Eighteenth. Hung Vuong had an extraordinarily beautiful daughter named Princess My Nuong. When My Nuong came of marrying age, Hung Vuong decided to have a contest to find the man most worthy of her hand. He invited great warriors, artists, writers, merchants and heroes from all over Vietnam. Among these men were two who stood out from all the rest: Son Tinh, who could raise mountains, and Thuy Tinh, who caused the sea to flood and the rains to fall.

When all these men were assembled before him, Hung Vuong realised that he had a problem: there were too many to choose from. So the Emperor decided to make things simple. He would send them all on a scavenger hunt. The first man to arrive back at the palace with one hundred plates of sweet rice, one elephant with nine tusks, one rooster with nine combs and one horse with nine red manes would get to marry the princess.

Son Tinh was the first to reach the capital with all of these amazing things. My Nuong was already dressed and waiting for him. With Hung Vuong's blessing, the two were married. Afterwards, they left right away for Son Tinh's home in the mountains.

Thuy Tinh was also able to find all the things the Emperor required, but he was too late and on arrival back at the palace he found that the Princess was already married. When Thuy Tinh learned that he'd lost the contest, he became furious, and set off to follow the newly-weds back to the mountains.

Thuy Tinh caused heavy rains to fall and the ocean to rise, nearly drowning Son Tinh and his new wife. But Son Tinh made the mountains rise higher and higher, carrying them out of reach of the raging waters. This went on until finally Thuy Tinh was exhausted and forced to admit defeat. He went back to his home in the ocean, still furious.

Today, these northern mountains where Son Tinh and My Nuong lived out their days are called the Mountain of the Lord and the Mountain of the Lady. Every year, Thuy Tinh tries once again to win the Princess back from his rival by unleashing terrible rainstorms and flooding the farmers' fields. But each year he fails, and his wrath grows ever stronger . . . and so, instead, Thuy Tinh takes his revenge on all those who accidentally fall into his grasp.

Prologue

O ne of my first memories of life is also my first memory of war.

I was five years old. My family was living in the small town of Ben Tre, just south of Saigon, which is now called Ho Chi Minh City. My father was a soldier in the Army of the Republic of Vietnam (ARVN). I barely knew him, as he was away much of the time, fighting in the jungle. My mother, my four-year-old sister Hanh and I lived in a military housing complex. This complex had twenty apartments to a floor. There was an army base nearby, so many of the families that lived with us were military. The base had sirens that were supposed to warn us of impending attacks, but they didn't always work, and when they did, they didn't always go off in time.

One day, Hanh and I were playing dressing-up in the bedroom. Like children anywhere in the world, this was one of our favourite games. My mother was well known for her skill at making *ao dai*, the long, flowing, traditional silk garments that Vietnamese women still wear today, and the closet was always full of her leftover scraps. We loved to drape ourselves in them, bowing to each other and pretending we were grown-up ladies.

Suddenly, there was a whistling, screeching sound overhead. Then there was another sound, a *boom!*, louder than anything I could have imagined. It shook the building, flinging debris and shrapnel against the walls and through the open windows. My mother and sister ran into the bathroom and hid. But I remained where I was, frozen with fear. What could have made such a noise?

I had no idea. I was as frightened as if the sky itself had fallen in.

If you've never been near a missile explosion before, you have no way of understanding the terror it causes. The shock waves cause the entire world to go wavy. Your entire body, for one hellish moment, turns to jelly. You wet your pants without even realising it, but you're too scared to be embarrassed. It's an experience that can traumatise anyone, even adults, for a lifetime. Imagine, then, the effect it would have on a five-year-old child. Later, it was explained to me that we had been under a missile attack. But I did not know either of the words 'missile' or 'attack'. All I knew was that it seemed like the world was ending and my mother was as frightened as we were.

I finally found my feet and ran into the bathroom, where my mother and sister were huddled in terror. On the roof of our apartment, there was a small concrete water reservoir in which we collected the monsoon rains. The three of us hid under this, hoping that it would offer some protection. This was a pathetic hope and we were perhaps putting ourselves in even more danger, as, had it fallen, it would certainly have crushed the three of us. But it was all we had.

The missiles continued to fly directly overhead for what seemed like an eternity. We heard every one of them, and we felt every explosion in our stomachs. We were just waiting for the one that would hit our building. But it never came.

About half an hour after the attack ended, we finally mustered up the courage to creep out of the bathroom and go outside to check the damage. Behind our building, there had been a house in which a family of two adults and three children lived. That house was now just a pile of rubble. The entire family had been huddled up in one room, hugging each other for protection, just as my mother and sister and I had done. Now they were all dead.

A crowd of us stood and watched in silence as their bloodied bodies were taken away on stretchers, one by one. We were stunned by the notion that death and destruction could drop out of the sky with no warning. We were also deeply frightened by the thought that it might happen again. I was too young to understand or know much about the war, but I knew who was attacking us – the Viet Cong, our so-called enemies. We were fighting against the North Vietnamese, or Ho Chi Minh, who were trying to invade South Vietnam.

This single experience would have been enough to change me for ever. But the attacks continued. Somehow, like all Vietnamese, Mother, Hanh and I learned to live in a constant state of fear. How did we do it? I have no answer to that, other than to say that humans are driven towards one thing: survival. Children, especially, are resilient and strong. When one's very life is at stake, there is no time for questions, thoughts or even tears. That comes later, when the fighting has stopped – sometimes years later.

That's why I'm writing this book. My name is Juliet Lac, and I am now forty years old. I am a single working mother, a website owner and a life-insurance specialist. These days, I write short stories for my website, which I conceived and designed for English-speaking women living in Paris. I am a lot of other things, too. But most importantly I am self-reliant and what I call 'stand-alone', by which I mean I can get by on my own, just as I have done since early childhood.

But I wouldn't ever have been any of these things if I hadn't been a survivor first. And deep down, underneath all the various labels I can apply to myself today, I am still a survivor. I am no longer that stunned and helpless five-year-old girl, but I can still feel her pain. And if that little girl had known what further hardships lay ahead of her as she watched the broken bodies of those children being taken away that day, she might just have given up right then and there.

Luckily for us, we can't see into the future. And it's always too late to change the past. All there is, is the moment: right now. This is what matters. This, and the sacredness of life.

Throughout the history of the human race, people have endured the storms of war and prospered in the lull of peace.

Some people, the unlucky ones, only ever get to experience pain and suffering. Others live out their lives without ever knowing a moment's turmoil. I, Juliet, have lived through both. Am I unlucky because of the terrible things that happened to me as a child, or am I lucky because of the life I live now? I hardly know myself. All I can tell you is that no sane person would ever choose war over peace. War is madness. It is inhuman. It's not about ensuring safety or prosperity, no matter what the politicians say. War is what people do to each other when they have completely forgotten the sacredness of life.

Many people who would never choose war – mothers, fathers, children, grandparents – are forced to live through it anyway. It's chosen for them by their leaders. It comes to them suddenly, a terrible monster with a ravenous appetite that can never be satiated.

For these people, who have lost everything, all they can do is run – or die.

My mother and I chose to run.

This is our story.

Part 1

Vietnam, 1967–78

1

Childhood

I was born on 5 August 1967, the child of a soldier and a seamstress. About the most insightful thing I can say about my parents is that they didn't get along with each other. Only now, looking back, do I see that they never could have. It's the job of soldiers to destroy, while seamstresses sew things back together. Forever at cross-purposes, their union was doomed from the start.

My mother, Suong, was probably twenty-two at the time of my birth, although because of poor record keeping she was never sure of the exact date of her birth. In addition to being known for her ao dai, she was also famed, in a local sense at least, for her great beauty – just as her mother had been before her. The Vietnamese prize women with slender figures, fair skin and delicate features. My mother possessed all of these qualities, but I didn't inherit any of them. Instead, I got her pride – and her survival skills.

My mother's family history is complicated. Her father was dead by the time she was born. He had been killed while my grandmother was pregnant – shot as a spy by Southern forces. He was suspected of being a supporter of Ho Chi Minh, so the family story goes, but there was a lot of finger pointing and accusations in those trying days. It required someone of influence to speak up on a person's behalf if they were to be spared the firing squad. In my grandfather's case, as I was told, he might have lived had the local Catholic priests been willing to vouch for him. Apparently, they had some evidence that he was innocent. But the priests refused to do this, supposedly because my grandfather had once been in training for the priesthood but had left the seminary after meeting and falling in love with the woman who would become my grandmother. As revenge, they let him die at the hands of his own countrymen.

Today, I don't know for sure if this story is true or not, but I grew up believing that it was, and I have no particular reason to doubt it. I have often wondered whether, if it hadn't been for the pettiness of those priests, the story of my family would have turned out much differently. We might have had a chance of normality, despite the fact that our country was in chaos. But, as it was, the execution of my grandfather was the start of our family's long, slow disintegration. My grandfather was not around to love, nurture and raise my mother. He was not there to see her through school or to advise her on the marriage arrangement with my father. He was not there to protect her when she needed him. Mother was born and grew up without a father's love and protection.

After her husband's death, my grandmother married a Chinese businessman named Thanh, with whom she had a further seven children. Thanh, who was technically my step-grandfather, had numerous other wives or mistresses, some in Saigon and others scattered about the country in various small towns. It is widely acceptable for a man in Vietnam to be married to one woman and still have several mistresses. These women sometimes know about each other and accept the situation as long as the man provides and cares for them and any children they might have by him. Sometimes, however, the wife and mistresses don't know about each other, because the man does not reveal his secret relationships outside of marriage.

My step-grandfather ran a movie theatre in our town called Rap Hat Lac Thanh – which means simply 'Thanh Lac's Theatre' – as well as various successful businesses in Saigon and Ben Tre. He was quite wealthy. I remember seeing him on the street sometimes when I was small, but I don't believe he ever knew who I was, and it's doubtful he would have cared if he had.

I don't know exactly how old my father was when I was born,

but he was most likely around the same age as my mother. His name was Nam. My parents' marriage was arranged by a relative of my grandmother, which was common in our culture. Father married my mother because she was beautiful; she married him because she had to marry someone and he seemed a likely protector. But this proved to be a forlorn hope, because he was never home. In Vietnam, it is common to rely heavily on the extended family for support, but because, as a military family, we moved around all the time, we were often separated from our relatives in my early childhood. Another reason was my parents' constant arguing and my father's bad treatment of my mother. My father was well known in his family for his quick temper, which unfortunately I have inherited in some ways. As a result of his harsh treatment towards my mother, she rarely took us to visit his family members. She also avoided talking about them, and this affected our lives and our relationships with my father's side of the family. For us to be cut off from everyone was a strange and empty feeling – almost like there was no place in the world we really belonged.

My name back then was not Juliet Lac but Dung Nguyen. Nguyen was the name of a famous king from ancient times, but we can claim no blood ties – not that it would have saved us anyway. Dung means 'beauty' in Vietnamese, but it has less pleasant connotations in English. Many years later, when I became an American citizen, I changed it to Juliet, a name I had always admired after reading the famous Shakespearean love story *Romeo and Juliet* in a French class during my freshman year in high school.

When I was just five months old, in January of 1968, the Communist forces launched a massive attack on several South Vietnamese provincial capitals and military bases. This became known as the Tet Offensive. 'Tet' is the Vietnamese word for New Year, which in Vietnam begins at the end of January. My mother, caught in the middle of the fighting, literally had to run for her

life many times. She clutched me to her breast as she dashed
through the rice fields in Ben Tre on her way home from a friend's
house. She hid from the Viet Cong – who would have killed both
of us in cold blood, mother and child, without hesitation – and
meanwhile also had to dodge falling bombs, which kill just as
indiscriminately. She would tell me later that it seemed like she
was always running in those days.

My father was running, too, somewhere in the jungle. We only
saw him once a year during his annual leave from the military,
and my memories of his visits are not happy ones. On one
occasion, when I was four years old and my sister was three, my
father came home with some friends from his unit after a long
time away in the jungle. They brought with them an assortment
of strange food I had never seen before, including a number of
insects. He told my mother to cook them a big dinner. Then he
and his friends started drinking. When he was good and soused,
my father put a fat yellow worm on my plate.

'Eat it!' he said. 'It's good!'

'What is it?' I asked, uneasy at both the worm and his
drunkenness.

'It's a coconut worm. A rare delicacy,' he told me. 'These worms
live at the tops of palm trees. They eat only coconuts, and they're
very hard to get. So don't waste it!'

I didn't want to eat it, but I had to, or he would have become
angry. In fact, it wasn't bad. It was creamy, like butter mixed with
coconut milk.

My father also brought home something else I had never seen
before: chocolate. He'd got it from some American soldiers. I
much preferred this to the coconut worm, and both my sister and
I clamoured for more.

It was a lively dinner. My father, to put it bluntly, was drunk,
and well into the evening he and my mother started arguing in
front of all of us. These arguments were commonplace whenever
he was home, and they were mostly about his failure to take
responsibility for his family and about his drinking, about his

lack of attention and love for his little girls, and about his quick temper. Naturally, Hanh and I found it very scary. Finally, my father threw my mother – and us kids – out of the house, so that he and his friends could continue their party uninterrupted by the annoying demands of his family.

We went down the street to our neighbours' and asked if we could stay with them, but late that night, my father came looking for us. I don't know if he was remorseful or looking to continue the fight, but he and my mother ended up having a loud argument in the street. Then, my father began chasing her around. Hanh and I were once again terrified. It wasn't enough that our country was at war. We couldn't even be sure that we were safe from the man who was supposed to love us and take care of us. It never occurred to us that he was only trying to scare our mother. We thought he was really going to hurt her. We were very afraid for our mother, who was all we had. And I have no doubt that my mother was afraid for her very life, too.

As to why no one else stepped in – well, it's difficult to explain life in a developing country at war to people who have never experienced it. There was chaos everywhere; everyone had problems. And in Vietnam, one minds one's own business. No one would have approved of my father's behaviour, but no one would have felt it was their place to interfere in an argument between a man and his wife, either.

We stayed up all night, Hanh and I. Early the next morning, we crept home again, afraid of what we might find. But when we pushed open the door, we breathed sighs of relief. Our mother was asleep in the family bed, alone. My father had disappeared – gone back to the war without a word of goodbye to any of us.

This wasn't unusual for him. Neither was his behaviour of the night before. My father had little love for us, so it seemed, and he always had a short temper. This, when coupled with his drinking, was the reason he was demoted several times during his service. It was also the reason why we lived in mortal fear whenever he was around.

My mother, Hanh and I continued to live alone. Many families were in the same predicament then, because nearly all of the available men were away fighting. Many young single women were fighting alongside them, too. In America, women were marching for equal rights, but in Vietnam they already had them – at least when it came to fighting and dying in the field. Few Vietnamese people had access to television then, but still, I wonder what the women of my country would have thought if they could have seen the women of America up in arms over things like birth control and unfair pay, when their own biggest worry was how to survive.

The result of this was that there were few people of my parents' age around in the local towns and villages. This is another effect of war – it takes the most energetic and productive of a nation's people, and it destroys them. Regardless of whether the war is 'won' or 'lost', many of those people are gone for ever, and there is simply no way of telling how much the world has missed out on because of it. The true cost of every war – even of every single unjust death, such as my grandfather's – is incalculable.

But the fact that we were all in the same boat didn't stop some people from trying to take advantage of others who were even more vulnerable than themselves. One night, as I lay half-asleep, I heard noises near our kitchen, which was open to the outside and therefore allowed easy access to our apartment. Someone was trying to break in. There was a locked door between the kitchen and our main living space, but the intruder managed to open it. The family bed was next to the door, and I heard everything. Of course, I pretended to be asleep. My mother, too, was fully awake but petrified with fear.

We lay there and listened to the burglar as he rummaged through our things. Despite my fear of him, I wished dearly that my father were there so he could protect us. I had never wanted him more than I did at that moment.

Whoever the thief was, he knew the layout of our place well. He went directly to our closet – which was where we kept everything of value – opened it and took most of its contents. Then he simply walked out the front door. For the rest of the night, Mother and I just continued to lie there, too frightened to move.

In the morning, my mother checked her possessions and found that all of her legal papers had been taken. These papers might not have seemed important to anyone else; however, a Viet Cong supporter could use my mother's identity in order to travel freely in and out of cities and villages nearby. A few days later, a neighbour came to tell her that they'd found some pieces of her identification in an empty apartment in the next complex over. Although I don't remember the exact details, I do remember that with this clue my mother knew instantly who had broken into our place: our downstairs neighbours.

It was a cruel realisation. We considered these people to be friends of ours, and they had been invited into our home many times. That was why the burglar knew his way around and exactly what he was looking for. My mother was even in the middle of making some ao dai for the women of the family. Unfortunately, she liked to brag about her valuable possessions to her clients. Pride was one of her great flaws. This time, it had come back to bite her.

But the real problem, of course, was that we didn't have a man in the house. In Vietnamese culture, this is essentially a catastrophe. Without a man for protection and income, a woman and her children are extremely vulnerable.

Being so young, I didn't know that there was anything unusual about my life. I thought everyone lived the way we did. But of course, growing up in a developing country, I would have experienced nothing of what Western people might call normality anyway. We had no electricity and therefore no refrigeration. Many Vietnamese of my generation are lactose-intolerant because they didn't consume dairy products when they were young – there was no cool place to store them. We had very limited access to medical care. The roads in our town were made of dirt and gravel, and my face would get covered with dust whenever a bus passed by. Our homes were small and there was no public sanitation. People regularly fell sick because of the dirty flies and other virus-carrying insects.

But some things remained constant, even in wartime. For instance, we got to go to school. When I was five, I attended an all-girls school that was about fifteen minutes' walk from our house. I always ran, because I was fearful that a missile attack might come at any moment. On average, we were attacked at least once a week – and the worst thing was to be caught out in the open.

There was an all-boys school just across the road, where my favourite aunt, Tuyet, my mother's older sister, was a teacher. We saw her when my mother took me to dinner with her family. She was a great cook, and I loved most of her authentic dishes.

Customarily, as a sign of respect, we had to bow our heads every time we walked in front of a teacher – even my dear aunt. Her name meant 'snow', which was something none of us had ever seen, but all the same it sounded wonderful to me. She used to give me new clothes every New Year. From Aunt Tuyet I learned a meticulous sense of cleanliness. Later, I would also learn from her that a woman can be self-reliant, independent and resourceful – but also that the more trust she extends, the more vulnerable she is. This would be illustrated in graphic detail just a few years later by what befell poor Tuyet.

At the entrance to my school, there was a gate with the school's name (which I don't remember) on a board placed near the top, and in the middle of the courtyard there was a tall pole from which hung the national flag. Every morning before class, we students were made to line up neatly under the flag and sing the national anthem. At the time, the Republic of South Vietnam's national flag had a yellow background with three red stripes in the middle. To me, these colours represented not freedom and independence but a tiny bit of routine and predictability, which are, after all, the things that make children feel secure. After the singing, everyone quietly filed into their rooms. The classrooms were built around the flagpole in a rectangular shape and divided into sections, according to the age of the pupils. I was assigned to a classroom to the north-east side, and I remember having lessons in maths, French and the Vietnamese language, among others.

In those days, all students had to wear crisp white shirts with either black trousers or knee-length skirts. I remained so small that I was able to wear the same shirt and skirt from the first through to the sixth grade. For many years, in fact, I neither grew nor gained weight, an indication of childhood malnutrition. But even though I was so small, dark and skinny, I was considered a bit fat when compared to other girls. Sometimes the girls as well as adults would tell me that I looked chubby, and this made me very unhappy.

Another possible sign of malnutrition was that I was very forgetful. I used the same ring binder for my maths, science and language classes, and I was always losing it. Then I would have to redo all my work, a source of immense frustration. Most of my teachers were annoyed by my stupidity and carelessness, and one day they called Mother to school to show her my bad work and discuss my study habits. They asked Mother to buy more binders for me and to try to keep an eye on my schoolwork at home. I wasn't a stupid child, but I was easily distracted. I did a lot of daydreaming, and my mind often seemed to wander. I was not good with textbooks or learning. But despite these problems, and living under constant bombardment and the daily fear of death, I was a happy little girl. I watched the adults around me accept and adapt to the life-and-death pattern of war, and so I thought that things must be OK. But I could not have been more wrong. I understood nothing. Looking back, though, I realise that this was probably for the best.

In our break time, if no citywide alarms had gone off, warning of an impending attack, we would go to play at a lake near the school. We would walk or run around it, enjoying the fresh air as we talked and played with each other – but always ready to take cover at any moment. The lake was a popular spot. Older people came there to do their daily exercises, and sometimes men fished for carp with long bamboo rods. People did their best to live normal lives, despite the fact that all across the country hundreds were dying every week in the most horrible ways.

Another nice place to visit was the boardwalk that ran along the Mekong River, further to the west. This was a more fashionable spot, with plenty of chic coffee bars and fancy cafés and restaurants. Here, you could walk leisurely along, just people-watching or enjoying the view. Or you could sit on benches to read and relax. Young lovers took romantic strolls alongside the sluggish muddy water and stole kisses, though stronger displays of public affection were frowned upon. My uncle – the third half-brother of my mother – took me to the river on a few occasions and bought me a smoothie at one of the coffee bars. This was a true delight, for it was a luxury my mother could not afford. I didn't realise it at the time, but I was serving as a cover for my uncle's visits to his girlfriend, who often came along with us. She was from a strict family, and I suppose my presence during their courtship prevented the possibility of things getting out of hand – as well as making my uncle look good.

One day at the river, I was playing with some of the floating waterweeds. I reached out to pick a wild flower and promptly fell in. I did not know how to swim, and I had no body fat to help me float. I began to sink immediately. I struggled hard, kicking and thrashing my arms and legs in mortal fear. A lot of the Mekong water went down my throat before my uncle finally pulled me up.

Since that day, I've had a real fear of water, and I quickly came to think of my first encounter with the Mekong as my first confrontation with Thuy Tinh, the ancient Vietnamese god of water. I was born under the astrological sign of Thuy, 'water', who in Vietnam is considered an angry spirit. My superstitious mother was always making comments about how my personality was like his: jealous and vengeful, always lashing out like a storm. Now I began to wonder if Thuy Tinh had somehow sensed my presence on the riverbank and tried to pull me in as a replacement for the beautiful Princess My Nuong, whose loss he still mourned.

In the future, I would make every effort to avoid water, so that Thuy Tinh wouldn't be able to grab me with his foaming fists. But my attempts were often in vain. Again and again, I would have to confront the angry god of the rivers and oceans and fight for my survival. As much as I would have liked to think of my first encounter with the Mekong as a kind of inoculation, guaranteeing me safe passage the next time I was in danger of drowning, in fact it was quite the opposite. It would seem that my brief visit to Thuy Tinh's realm had only allowed him to get a taste for me. He would try again and again to drag me down to his watery kingdom . . . and it would require every ounce of strength in my tiny body to fend him off.

2

The War

Like many survivors of war, a large part of my childhood is lost to me. I don't just mean that I didn't have a normal life, brought up in a safe and secure environment. I mean that there are big chunks of memory missing. But sometimes these missing chunks come back to me in strange flashes – usually when I am in the middle of doing something else, like washing the dishes or driving home after a long day at work. It's as if these memories are desperate to be reclaimed, despite the fact that there is a very good reason I tried to shut them away for ever. Like insistent children who won't take no for an answer, they wait until I am distracted before they try to sneak back into my consciousness. If there's one thing I've learned from this, it's that one cannot keep things buried for ever. It's like trying to hold a bunch of balloons underwater. Eventually, you're going to get tired, and they'll start popping up one by one – so you might as well just let them all go.

One image that came back to me often over the years is of Mother, Hanh and me walking down a dirt road in a place I don't recognise. We're in a village somewhere in the mountains. It's grey and cold, and the wind seems to slice through my waiflike body like a sword through paper. Being from much further south and a much lower elevation, cold is an unfamiliar sensation to me. I hate it. I feel chilled and sick. All around us are soldiers, both American and South Vietnamese, and there are other people, too, strange-looking people of a kind I have never seen before. These people are selling vegetables at roadside stands. They are neither Vietnamese nor African-American soldiers, whom I saw when

Mother took me to Saigon. Everyone ignores us, and my mother is not speaking to Hanh or me either. She walks along as if in a daze, not caring whether we follow or not.

That memory had always puzzled me, because it never seemed to fit with any others. It wasn't until I was writing this book in my home in Paris that I was finally able to determine where it belonged in my life. It was early in 1975. The strange-looking people were 'mountain people' – Hmong tribesmen, who are ethnically different from the rest of the Vietnamese people.

And then I remembered: we were going to Pleiku, in the central highlands of Vietnam, to identify my father's body.

The last time I'd seen my father had been some weeks earlier. He'd just finished another drunken, aggression-filled spree at home with us. Before he left to return to his unit – and uncharacteristically for him – he'd stood, just for a moment, in the street below our apartment, looking up at us. My sister and I were leaning out of the window, looking down at him. I don't recall any particular expression or gesture of sadness on his part. It was as if we were strangers staring at each other across a crowded room. After a while, he simply turned and walked away, without so much as a wave – just as he always did. We watched him go with no more than idle curiosity and probably a sense of relief. I wonder if I would have felt any different if I'd known it was the last time I would ever see him alive.

A few days after he left, someone in the village came to inform my mother of a terrible fact. My father, it turned out, had another wife and children elsewhere in Vietnam. Enraged, my mother left Hanh and me to fend for ourselves – something she did quite often – and set out to find the truth. During the days that she was away, Hanh and I went to my Uncle Hieu's house, located a few yards away. We ate with his family, and at night we slept over with our cousins – we were lucky to have them living very close to our house. When Mother returned home some days later, I remember she was crying. We knew better than to ask what this meant: obviously the rumour was true.

Hanh and I were more confused than upset by this news. Since our day-to-day lives remained unaffected, we just brushed it off. Being little girls, we didn't understand the real implications it held for our mother. Then, just a few days later, while she was still crying over my father's infidelity, we learned that he had been killed in action.

This in itself was not unexpected, given his occupation. But it was a blow nonetheless, especially coming on top of the news that he had been unfaithful – not just to my mother but to all of us. Suddenly, I understood why my father had never shown us any love – because he had another family whom he must have loved more. I wondered if there was a little girl my age in that family, one who was pretty instead of ugly, well behaved instead of stubborn and petty. It all made sense to me now. We were the bad family, the mistake family. I was the daughter he wished he'd never had; Mother was the wife he wished he'd never married.

Yet there was no time to process our hurt feelings. We had to go and claim the body if we wanted to have a funeral – and not to have a funeral was to risk incurring the wrath of my father's ghost. His spirit already had reason to be outraged, as he had been killed by a traitor, a Communist sympathiser in his own unit who had apparently set off some kind of bomb that had blown my father and some other men to bits.

The army typically gathered the bodies of fallen soldiers and placed them in a kind of collection centre, where families had to come and make a positive identification before they could be released for burial. Of course, I was not allowed to see my father's corpse. That was my mother's terrible task. But she told me later that he was scarcely recognisable, not just as her husband but even as a human being. Such was the awful damage that the bomb had done to his body. When she came back from viewing his body, my mother seemed frozen and empty, like a zombie. I felt cold and blank.

We went back home in the back of an army truck, but I remember little about the journey, as I soon fell asleep. When we arrived, my mother and my father's close relatives cleaned what was left of his body and put it in a coffin, along with his most treasured personal belongings. They took all the buttons off his clothing, because it was believed that buttons are painful to spirits in the next world. Then we closed the coffin and put it in the middle of our house, where it was to remain for the next few days as friends and family members came to pay their respects. Part of me wondered if my father's other family would appear – much as I dreaded meeting them, I was also curious about who they were – but they never did.

My family was officially Catholic, and Mother had both me and Hanh baptised out of respect for her father's sisters, who were all nuns. But because of what the priests had done to my grandfather – or rather, because of what they had failed to do for him – we didn't go to church any longer, and there were strong elements of older religions in our lives. So, there was nothing Catholic about my father's funeral, except the fact that he was to be buried instead of cremated. Everyone wore white clothes and wrapped white scarves around their heads, because in our culture white is the colour of death and mourning. Then a large metal bowl was placed on the floor. My relatives burned fake money in it, so that my father would have something to spend as he established his new life in the other world. We placed a small table at the head of the coffin. On this was placed my father's photo, incense, tea and flowers.

It was very hot, and after his body had been in the house for two days it began to smell. So we had the funeral a day early. We performed a ceremony at home and then walked in a procession to the cemetery. The family went in front, holding a picture of my father, and the coffin rode behind on a camion. When we finally reached the cemetery, I saw that it was old and neglected. Some of the forgotten graves had been dug up, exposing the coffins inside. Others had been robbed and left open, and they looked to me like the gaping maws of ravenous monsters.

Although I cried when we buried my father, I don't recall that his death actually brought me much sadness. In fact, I hardly remembered who he was. To me, he was a cold and distant figure whom I was not allowed to touch, and who, on those rare occasions when he was home, would get drunk and terrorise my mother, laughing at her screams. He never brought us presents; never let us sit on his lap. And whenever he left us to go back to the army, it was without a single word of farewell, without a single tender gesture. At the time, he seemed like nothing more than a scary stranger to whom we were obliged to show respect.

But now, as a grown woman, when I remembered our trip to Pleiku and then thought about his funeral, I was filled with sadness as I thought about what my father's short life must have been like. Perhaps he wouldn't let us sit on his lap because he knew that sooner or later he was going to be killed, and then his loss would have been all the harder on us. And if he had let himself love us, he would never have wanted to go back to the war. No sane person chooses war – and war had taken my father's humanity long before it killed him. I am not saying that my father was insane. What I mean is that he was already only half a person. As happens to many soldiers, his soul had already left him long before his body was destroyed. As I sat in that room in Paris with my memories, I felt a flood of love for my father and I missed him terribly. I finally came to realise the pain that he must have gone through and admired the courage that had enabled him to hide his true feelings. Rather than the monster of my early memories, I realised that he was, after all, only human like everyone else, and I started to forgive him for all that he had done to my mother, Hanh and me.

My father was not even thirty when he died. He would likely have had little or no understanding of the real causes of what Americans called the Vietnam War but which we eventually came to call the American War. He was caught up in it and sacrificed, like two million or more other Vietnamese, on the altar of idealism. Human nature demands that we try to find some meaning in such a senseless waste of life. At the age of forty, I came to think that at least the war showed other people in the world they could fight against their oppressors and win – for I, like many Southern Vietnamese, was not unsympathetic to the anti-colonial sentiments of Ho Chi Minh. I respect what he tried to do for our country. Our country and its people had been under the control of foreigners for so long. It was time to stand up, speak out and fight for our freedom and the right to rule our own country without any foreign influence or involvement. In my opinion, Ho Chi Minh was a man of intelligence, courage and determination. He was a great leader, apart from his adoption of Communist beliefs. But did the Westerners give him any other choice?

At other times, however, I wonder if that whole terrible period was in vain, just a meaningless slaughter that served the political interests of foreigners who knew nothing of the real price that was being paid by us, the people of Vietnam.

3

After the War

In April 1975, Saigon fell and the war finally ended, with our enemies, the Communists, the victors. Vietnam was once again unified, and the new leaders began to impose their harsh dictates on the entire population. I was eight that year, old enough to remember plenty of details – but again, many things are lost to me. And an eight-year-old girl has no understanding of politics. I knew only that, even though the fighting had stopped, the suffering was continuing – for Vietnamese people in general, and for my family in particular.

My mother sank into a deep depression after my father's death. Although their marriage had been marked by unhappiness and lengthy separations from each other, at least she was still under the nominal protection of a male. As I have mentioned earlier, this is still important in Vietnamese society, which, for better or worse, has managed to retain many of its ancient traditions. Now, once her mourning period of three months was over, my mother would have to find a new husband. This prospect seemed to sadden her – not out of loyalty to my father but because she believed that men in general were untrustworthy and brutal. This had been her experience of them so far, and she had no reason to believe that things were going to be any different now.

Of course, my mother had never been a happy person to begin with. Her life was destined to be difficult before it even started, following the execution of her father. And as in many Asian cultures, she was at a disadvantage because she was a girl. Female children are not valued as highly as males. Girls are considered a liability, while boys are an asset. My mother's brother and half-brothers received preferential treatment while she was either ignored or spoken to harshly and made to do extra work around the house.

Yet despite all this, my mother still prayed for boy children for herself. I think she had wanted four children altogether, as she once told me that she had four names picked out. They were based on an old Vietnamese proverb: *Cong Nhan Dung Hanh,* or Hard Work, Value, Beauty, Gentleness. I was Beauty. Hanh was Gentleness. The boys never arrived.

My name was ironic, for according to all who knew me I was anything but beautiful, both inside and out. My own female relatives often made disparaging comments about my dark skin and heavy features, especially my thick lips. And my mother said that I was jealous of Hanh from the time she was an infant, even going as far as to steal her bottle and drink her French powdered milk myself. Most people liked Hanh more than me. She was both Beauty and Gentleness: she listened when people spoke to her, and she obeyed when told to do something. In Vietnam, obedience and respect are among the most desirable qualities a girl can have. I, on the other hand, was rebellious, selfish and wilful.

I had a difficult relationship with my mother from as far back as I can remember. I felt she was always complaining about me, and I would yell at her in retaliation. I often snapped at her and spoke to her rudely, and this was seen as terrible behaviour. Hanh behaved like an angel compared to me, so it was no wonder that she seemed to be more popular.

One day, about three months after the war ended, my sister, who was then seven years old, rinsed herself off in the shower with the rainwater that had collected in the rooftop reservoir. There was nothing unusual about this – this was what the reservoir was for. But immediately afterwards, she complained of feeling feverish. At first, we weren't worried, but then her temperature began to mount. Within a few hours, Hanh had fallen unconscious.

My mother took her immediately to the nearby hospital. But the Communists, in their infinite wisdom, had already sent most of the doctors to their so-called 're-education camps' (if torture and death by starvation can be considered a form of education). This meant that there was no one left who was qualified to diagnose what was ailing Hanh, only nurses, orderlies and janitors. She never had a chance.

My sister regained consciousness on her own that night, only to begin vomiting blood and tiny pieces of intestine. Nobody was able to do anything to help her. They didn't even have the training to tell my mother what was wrong.

By midnight, little Hanh was dead.

I had been left home alone. I spent the entire night sitting at the window – the same one through which Hanh and I had looked down at our father for the last time. It was an unusually cold night for South Vietnam, with lots of wind and rain. Very early in the morning, my mother and her sister-in-law arrived on a mobilette, which was what we called the little motorised scooters that are urban Vietnamese people's main form of transportation. On my mother's lap was a form wrapped from head to toe in a white sheet. I knew at once that it was my sister's body. I stayed where I was, watching in disbelief through the raindrops that rolled down the windowpane as they carried her, limp and lifeless, into the house. All I could think of, in that moment, was how the thunderous downpour reminded me of the god of rains, rivers and oceans. It was as if Thuy Tinh was mocking me, showing me that if he couldn't get me, he would take those closest to me instead.

I was inconsolable. Despite what my mother said about me being jealous of Hanh, I had always loved my sister dearly. She was my best friend and constant companion. We played together, laughed and cried together, and even slept next to each other in the big family bed. In many ways, we were like one person. And my jealousy towards her had never been based on any ill will. It was only the normal kind of resentment that small children have when they feel they have been replaced in their parents' affections by a younger sibling.

There was one incident that had occurred some years earlier, which, after Hanh's death, I could not seem to stop replaying in my mind. My mother had gone out, and we decided that we were going to do some cooking, so we got into the sweet French powdered milk that we both loved so much and began mixing it with water. The result was predictable: a huge mess everywhere. When my mother came home, she was very angry. I pointed at Hanh and said that she had done it all by herself. My mother believed me; Hanh got spanked, and I got off scot-free. But she never said a word to Mother about my own guilt. She simply accepted all of the punishment that should have been half mine.

I have few true regrets in this life, but one of them is that incident. To this day, I remember it with shame.

Another regret is that I never told my sister I loved her. I don't feel the same amount of shame over this, for love is a word that was never used in our house, and that was not our fault. Yet I like to think that Hanh knew I loved her anyway.

I am certain that she knows it now.

After Hanh's death, my mother and I went into a tailspin. We were like two leaves fluttering helplessly, caught in the winds of winter. We became numb and emotionally frozen – to the world and to each other.

And yet, we had scarcely even begun to experience all the trials that life was to throw our way.

In 1976, with nowhere else to go and no one to take care of us, my mother and I moved in with her younger half-brother, Hong. Half-Uncle Hong had been born disabled in Ben Tre, though he was not as badly affected as his younger brother, Long, who could not talk or sit still, and who could not control the movements of his arms and legs. His mouth was always wide open, with spittle dribbling down the side. He was kept in a fixed high chair and had to be fed and bathed by my grandmother or a full-time caretaker.

Half-Uncle Hong had two tiny little legs that hadn't grown with the rest of him, but he could sit still and do things for himself. He was confined to a wheelchair, but this didn't stop him from living as full a life as possible. He ran a grocery store that was named after him, the Grocery Lac Hong, in a house that was owned by his father, Thanh, the wealthy Chinese businessman.

The house was tiny, with only two rooms. In the front room, facing the street, was the grocery store. Here, Half-Uncle Hong sold dried foods, such as peas and rice, as well as various household supplies. The dry goods were kept in their original sacks, with only the top opened and rolled down to display what was inside, and Half-Uncle Hong would measure out the amount that the customer requested into a smaller bag. They were neatly lined up on the floor. There were some racks on the walls of the shop where household supplies were kept, such as personal hygiene products and rare imported French goods for babies, like powdered milk, which was very popular in Vietnam. I sometimes sneaked in to eat a spoon or two of the wonderful sweetened raw powder. It smelled delicious and tasted like heaven.

The back room was a loft, which was further divided into a living room, a kitchen and two bedrooms. The bathroom was very simple, with a small tub that held the water. The toilet was a ceramic bowl built into the floor. There was no bathtub, no washing bowl or toilet seat like in Western countries.

Before and during the war, my half-aunts and half-uncles had lived there together. But now, since the Communists had confiscated the movie theatre, which was their main source of income, they had all moved to Ho Chi Minh City.

Needless to say, as payment for our room and board, my mother and I were expected to help run the store. But I did not find this too demanding a task, since Mother did most of the household chores for all of us. When I wasn't at school, I only had to watch the shop when she ran out to do errands or was cooking in the back room. The shop opened at 9 a.m., which was the hour that all the outdoor markets opened. Nobody in Ben Tre had refrigerators then, so people bought their food fresh every morning and cooked it that day. All around us were stalls selling Vietnamese-style pancakes – made with rice flour, coconut milk, onions, shrimp and pork – as well as rice-noodle soup and other delicious hot noodle dishes.

The grocery remained open until late in the evening, as did most of the hot food stalls. It was a loud, filthy neighbourhood, and it was often hard for me to sleep. At night, across the alley, a middle-aged woman sold homemade soups and hot rice dishes with fried duck. I could smell her food from the bed that I shared with Mother, and I often longed to cross over the stacks of trash that separated me from her delicious world. But by this time, I had become a shy and withdrawn little girl, and I hardly dared to speak to her or anyone else.

It was around this time that I discovered a way to escape from the inner pain that the loss of my sister had caused me: reading. My half-aunts and -uncles had left a number of books behind. I discovered them on a shelf one day, picked one up out of idle curiosity and was instantly hooked. The first one I read was a romantic novel by a famous Chinese writer named Quynh Dao. I also delved into the Chinese kung-fu action-adventure stories, which were then very popular in Vietnam and which are, with the success of such movies as *Hero* and *Crouching Tiger, Hidden Dragon*, becoming better known in the West today. These books were all written in an archaic style and seemed to me much like Shakespeare seems to a speaker of modern English. They were hard to understand, but I taught myself to decipher them, and soon I was able to read them with no problem. I was proud of this accomplishment, for I'd never been considered a particularly fast learner. This was the first time I had really set my mind to teaching myself how to do something, and I succeeded easily. So, these books brought me double pleasure. They provided an escape from the loneliness and sadness of my real life, and they also gave me the satisfaction of knowing that I was not, after all, just a dumb girl.

The love stories made me cry constantly. Sometimes I would read for hours, without eating or sleeping. My mother didn't seem to mind. Besides going to school, I had nothing else to do and no friends to play with. To most kids of my age who lived in and around the area, I was seen as a difficult little girl to be friends with. I hardly smiled or talked to anyone, even the adults. I always seemed to have a grouchy look on my face, and I often kept my head down and tried to ignore those around me as I retreated further and further into my own little world.

My duties at the shop were simple, like watching out for customers while my mother was out, dusting the shelves, picking up the peas and rice that fell on the floor and mopping the floors. I dreaded having to deal with customers, especially after one incident that occurred with a local boy whom I often saw at the boys' school across from mine. His father was one of the Communist leaders in town. One day, the boy came into the shop and asked to buy some rice, but Mother was out running her errands, so I told him to come back later. He was a bit angry and said that I was very rude. In turn, I then felt offended and answered him back snappily.

The boy got really angry at my bad attitude towards a customer. He turned around and left the store yelling, 'I will never come back to buy anything in this shop, and I will tell my father what you said!'

Although, thankfully, there were no repercussions as a result of this incident, after that I avoided having anything to do with customers.

Instead, I preferred to withdraw into my new world of romance and adventure. And my mother, for her part, was already absorbed with the first of what would become a long string of boyfriends, all of whom would be indifferent to me, and all of whom were only interested in my mother for her good looks. I met a few of these men when she invited them home to dinner, or when they came to see her to talk over a drink. But most of these relationships were very short-lived, and as a result I did not really try to get to know any of the men. I was happy in my own little world with my books and felt safe there, removed from reality.

During those rare moments when I wasn't reading, I amused myself in other ways. With all the food stalls surrounding us and no proper public sanitation, the area we lived in was a health inspector's nightmare. (There were no actual health inspectors, of course.) There were large piles of trash and rotting food everywhere. Sometimes, I simply sat and watched the flies as they swarmed over the garbage, buzzing and breeding to their hearts' content. They were the only creatures who thrived amidst the poverty and chaos.

One day, as I was staring in stupefaction at this seething dark mass of humming wings and shiny black bodies, a naked woman ran by the window. This might have seemed like an interesting distraction to a stranger, but I scarcely bothered to glance up. Everyone knew this poor lady was crazy, but there were no resources or facilities under the Communists to help people like her, so she was simply allowed to run the streets as if she was a mad dog.

She had plenty of company. War always leaves a swathe of cripples, orphans and mad people in its wake. I believe one may judge the quality of a society by how it treats its most helpless members. On this count, and many others, the Communists proved conclusively that, despite their self-professed idealism, any sense of the sacredness of life was lost to them for ever.

Life under this new regime was much harder. Rules and regulations were stricter. Everyone had to report to the local government to confirm their address and how many people were living there. No one was allowed to travel without a written permit from the authorities or to stay at different places or other households for more than one night. Local inspectors could knock on the door at any time to check the legal papers and permits of guests staying in the house. Children were taught to watch and report any suspicious activities of people around them, even those of their parents and loved ones. You were not allowed to say anything negative about the government, otherwise you ran the risk of being thrown into jail and punished without any fair trial. People disappeared mysteriously. We had to endure daily preaching about Communism from the authorities through loud speakers stationed on moving vehicles. Everyone became strangely quiet and cautious, and there were spying, prying eyes everywhere.

Our grocery store was just a few blocks away from my wealthy Chinese step-grandfather's former cinema. Step-Grandfather Thanh had survived the war, but the movie theatre was now under the control of the Communists, which was why all my aunts and uncles had fled to the city.

Communists fear independent thought; they always struggle to control the kind and quality of ideas that people encounter in their daily lives. So, the nature of the films that were shown there had changed drastically since the fall of Saigon. In the film *Good Morning, Vietnam*, Robin Williams takes his Vietnamese girlfriend to a cinema to see *Beach Blanket Bingo*, which featured Annette Funicello bopping around on the California sand in a bikini. Such displays of Western decadence, once common, were now outlawed. They were replaced with films that featured good old-fashioned Communist values. This meant that most of them were boring and full of propaganda.

I was allowed to go to the cinema whenever I wanted, but whereas before I had loved the glimpses it afforded me into the outside world, convincing me that there was a better life elsewhere, where I might fall in love with someone like the famous French actor Alain Delon, now there wasn't much I wanted to see.

But there was another reason to stay out of the cinema: ghosts.

Superstition is a major part of Vietnamese culture, especially when it comes to the spirits of the dead. My mother and her friends often communicated with the spirit world using a kind of Ouija board, on which ghostly messages were spelled out one letter at a time. I myself believed fully in ghosts and was always taking pains not to offend them.

Mother told me that during the Tet Offensive, a large number of people had hidden in the cinema. The Viet Cong found them and killed them all. My half-uncles and -aunts, who had continued to work in the cinema up until the fall of Saigon, said that they had often heard and seen all kinds of spooky noises and apparitions following that terrible event. After hearing this story, I always had the feeling that those helpless victims were watching me, silently imploring me to help them, and it was a feeling I was never able to shake. But I was desperate to escape the world around me, so occasionally I plucked up my courage and went to the cinema anyway, taking my seat among the phantoms, trying to ignore the tingling on my arms and the back of my neck as they plucked at me with their ethereal fingers.

Not all the films were bad. They showed *Dr Zhivago* and *Lawrence of Arabia*, which I thought were wonderful stories. There was another one I particularly liked, a Russian story about a male mermaid who is persecuted by humans, falls in love with a human woman and takes her to live with him in his watery kingdom. I was especially attracted to the underwater scenes. Perhaps this was because the characters were somehow managing to survive in an environment in which, by all rights, they should have been dead – which I compared to my own situation. Or perhaps it was because these tall, pale-skinned Russians seemed to be immune to Thuy Tinh and his raging desire for revenge.

If that was the case, then how I envied them.

I cannot say that my mother and I were particularly happy or unhappy during this time. Emotionally speaking, we were too numb to feel much of anything. Like many Vietnamese, we were surviving, and that was all. The war had taken a terrible toll on everyone, victors and conquered alike. For the next twenty years, the entire population would be picking itself up, brushing the dust off and proceeding with life as best as possible under the circumstances.

My mother continued to run Half-Uncle Hong's shop in the

morning. Then, in the evenings, she earned a little extra money by selling sweet coconut-milk desserts on the street outside the cinema. I went through the motions of going to school and then came directly home every day without stopping to play with anyone and remained engrossed in my books.

I did not learn much at school. I now found the lessons boring because most of them were about Communism and the Soviet Union. We were constantly being told how we young students should behave: obey Uncle Ho, as we were to call Ho Chi Minh, and serve the new government. I kept myself apart from the other children and said very little to my teachers. But my behaviour went largely unremarked upon, as it was such a difficult time of adjustment for most people. Everyone in our little town seemed to be uncertain of the future.

Self-pity is a dangerous and destructive emotion, but after what we had been through there was no way to avoid it – we thought of little except that which we had lost. I missed my beloved sister Hanh and, surprisingly, my father, too. Darkness threatened to consume us, every one, but I was so caught up in my own pain that I didn't give any thought to how terrible my mother's burden must have seemed to her, how sad and desperate she must have felt.

Yet it was about to get worse – much worse. And, like one of the other great losses we had experienced, it was presaged by news of more unfaithfulness.

My mother's beloved older sister and my favourite aunt, Tuyet – the one who had taught at the boys' school – had moved to Ho Chi Minh City after the war ended. As one of the few members of my family who had ever shown me any kindness, I missed her very much. But I was happy for her success. Aunt Tuyet had begun a small soy sauce manufacturing business that was expanding and doing well. Things were looking bright for her. But then Aunt Tuyet discovered that her husband was having numerous affairs.

To the best of my understanding, there's a fine line between adultery and polygamy in Vietnam. It's more accurate to call these other women mistresses rather than wives, but essentially 'wife' is what they are, even to the point where they bear children. In many Asian cultures, it's a sign of prosperity for a man to be able to maintain more than one household, just as it was for the Chinese noblemen of ancient – and not-so-ancient – times, as was the case with my Chinese step-grandfather Thanh.

But there are certain rules that must be followed. A husband must consult his wife before taking a mistress; to do otherwise is a sign of great disrespect. Just as my father did not do this with my mother, nor did my uncle with Aunt Tuyet. In our case, I sometimes wondered if my mother was the other woman, but if that had been so then his other family would have buried my father. Tragically, my aunt was unable to deal with the pain my uncle's disrespect had caused her, and late in 1976 Tuyet took her own life. She left behind two children, a newborn boy and his much older sister.

We went to Ho Chi Minh City for yet another funeral. I hated this journey even under pleasant circumstances, for the buses we took were old, rickety and always listed dangerously to one side or another, threatening to topple over into the ditch. Along both sides of the road were people selling fresh local food and fruit. These poor country women and men stood on the roadside holding one or two baskets of fresh fruit and juice drinks and begged the bus passengers to buy something. Sometimes they would run after the buses, desperate for someone to buy their goods. Most of them wore *ao ba ba*, traditional silk pyjamas, and *non la*, the famous Vietnamese conical hats that kept out the rain and provided shade from the sun.

The journey took about two to three hours, because we had to cross the Mekong River by a very slow ferry. Luckily, we did not have to stay on the bus while it was loaded up onto the ferry, but we were free to wander about the deck.

Once we arrived in the city, my uncle refused to acknowledge the emotional distress his infidelity had caused, which further enraged my already devastated mother. There was a lot of arguing, finger pointing and recrimination before my dear, beautiful aunt was buried in a rice field outside the city, and Mother and I went home, now more grief-stricken than we had imagined possible. My aunt's suicide was the source of a major rift in our family, with some people taking Tuyet's side and others taking my uncle's. As my mother was so clearly on Tuyet's side, I never saw her husband or her children again.

In less than two years, we had lost three of the most important people in our lives. It seemed that fate was determined to slowly whittle away at every last thing we considered dear and precious. Added to this pain was the fact that we had been on the losing side of a long and bitter civil war, and were now under the thumb of the people who had tried many times to kill us, who had killed my father in combat, and who had been responsible for the death of my little sister through their stupidity and arrogance. I felt numb and empty, and I was unable to cry – I had no more tears.

Then, in 1977, the Communists went one step further and took away the last of the property we had left: the house in which we lived and from which we helped run Half-Uncle Hong's little store. They argued that all wealth belongs equally to the people, so all property must be equally divided and shared. In my opinion, the Communists were not too different from thieves, as they stole wealth from the people through laws of their own making.

Communist ideology states that private ownership of property leads to moral decadence, bad values and the general decay of society. It is not right, they believe, for a few wealthy and powerful people to prosper, while the workers suffer and live in poverty. It's a belief that crystallised in Russia in the middle of the nineteenth century and since then has spread around the world, to various places where workers have felt themselves to be oppressed and unfairly treated.

In Vietnam, the Communists could point to the disastrous colonial influence of the French as the main reason why their way was clearly the best, and there was a great deal of truth in what they said. I have the impression that many Westerners believe that the French didn't come to Vietnam until the 1950s, but in fact they arrived a century earlier – ironically, at around the same time as Marx and Engels were writing the *Communist Manifesto*. The French presence in our country resulted in the enrichment of white European upper-class residents and aristocratic Vietnamese families, while depriving the vast majority of Vietnamese people of the natural resources that were theirs by birthright, as well as the fair value of their labour. In 1941, Ho Chi Minh, the French-educated son of a Confucian scholar who had been living abroad for several years, returned home to Vietnam and began the long struggle for Vietnam's independence from France.

No one who believes in freedom and equality can argue that this struggle in itself was a bad thing, in principle. After all, it was a nearly identical philosophy that led to America declaring its independence from Great Britain nearly two centuries earlier. But it was the supporters of Uncle Ho, as he is called, and most especially the Viet Cong, who demanded that the blood of all who opposed them flow through the streets, and who mercilessly destroyed not only the soldiers of the South but also their homes and families.

There is no doubt that, as Ho Chi Minh said, 'Nothing is more precious than independence and liberty.' Both the American Constitution and Declaration of Independence are based on these precise principles. In fact, the war in Vietnam was not a clear-cut black-and-white issue, for there were many Southerners who shared Ho's goal of an independent Vietnam. They just didn't see why Communism, and in particular the violent Viet Cong version of Communism, was the only alternative.

And there can also be no doubt that the Vietnamese Communists, like Communists everywhere, are nothing more than hypocrites, liars and murderers, who are ultimately interested only in the same thing capitalists are interested in: personal gain and the propagation of their own world view. Communists, for all their ideological fervour, are just as susceptible to bribery and corruption as everyone else. The natural urge to accumulate wealth is not eradicable through forced re-education or even outright murder but is a basic part of the human psyche.

What does this mean in plain English? It means that my family's cinema and store were confiscated because in theory they posed a risk to Communist values but in practice because they were another source of revenue that the government could take for itself, enriching top party officials and keeping the rest of the people poor – just like the hated French had done before them.

We, the people, were no longer allowed to own anything of great value. But the Viet Cong had no problem with my mother using her pathetic savings to buy a small piece of property in an area where there was no economic development or infrastructure, and therefore no wealth for them to exploit (in the name of non-exploitation). So, with her unerring instinct for survival, that was what Mother did: she bought a piece of land hours away from anywhere, and hired some locals to build us a house.

For the umpteenth time in my life, we were moving.

My half-uncle moved in to live with my grandmother and his disabled brother Long. But my mother and I left Ben Tre altogether. We bid farewell to Half-Uncle Hong and moved to the middle of nowhere – deep into the countryside, the last place in Vietnam we felt safe.

4

Wild Child

Our new home was in a place formerly called Huu Dinh – I don't recall what the Communists renamed it. The village was about one or two hours north of Ben Tre towards Saigon by bus. For miles and miles in every direction, there was nothing to see but palm trees and rice paddies. The house had a tall foundation, which was made of mud that had been collected from two nearby small rivers. Its roof and walls were constructed from corrugated metal. There was one large bedroom, one large front room and a nice-sized kitchen. A back door led to the garden, where we grew a few vegetables and herbs for cooking. Just outside that door was the shower, surrounded with a plastic sheet. One of the rivers ran in front of our house, the other out the back. We washed our clothes and dishes in the back river. A fallen palm tree served as a bridge over the front river and allowed us access to the road, which was little better than a dirt footpath and was frequently a sea of mud.

My mother's older brother, Hieu, whose name means something like 'respectful to one's parents', had also left the city and moved with his family to a place near ours. But 'near' is a relative term in the boondocks. Uncle Hieu's new home was actually about three hours' walk from ours – and walking was the only way we could get anywhere. Our nearest neighbours were much closer: one family lived across the back river and another was just a few palm-tree bridges down from ours. Besides them, there were no other houses in view.

I was now ten years old, and I was more unhappy than I had

5

ever been. The main reason for my unhappiness was the isolation I felt at being so far away from everything and everyone that I knew. My mother was often away in the city, as she had found a new line of work: selling jewellery. Many of her half-siblings, the children of wealthy Step-Grandfather Thanh, owned jewellery shops in Saigon. From them, she purchased various pieces – usually diamonds – at a discounted rate and then sold them to clients in the city at regular prices, thus earning herself a small profit. It was another typically ingenious move by a woman who would always find a way to keep her head above water. I also think that she needed to be surrounded by the excitement and bustle of a city; and her primary focus was always on surviving and prospering.

The problem with this for me was that she was gone for days or weeks at a time, and this meant I was expected to fend for myself. I wasn't completely alone, as a young man who was related to me somehow – I never knew exactly how – came to live with us. His name was Hung, which means 'courage' or 'strength'. He was about twenty-two years old, tall and as strong as his name implied. Also, he had dark skin like mine. Hung had spent his entire life in the countryside, moving from village to village and doing I have no idea what to support himself. He was a complete stranger to me, and I'm not sure my mother had even met him before she invited him to live in our house. But, as unthinkable as this situation might sound to Western readers, it would have been even more unthinkable for us not to have had Hung there as a form of male protection.

I thought of complaining to my mother about how lonely I felt, but in the end I didn't bother. There was no one to listen except Hung, and he didn't care; and even if he had, there was nothing he could have done about it.

On some of her visits home, Mother brought her boyfriend Nhon with her. This was the man who had sold her the land that we were living on. She seemed to like him a lot, and they talked and laughed together for hours. She cooked some special dishes, like thinly sliced beef wrapped in local leaves then grilled on an outdoor open fire. We ate this outside like a picnic. Nhon was a nice man and he treated me kindly. One time he took my mother and me to see his two young sons, Toai and Nguyen, who lived with his mother whenever he was away from home, as he was separated from his wife. His house was about two hours' walk from ours. His mother was a very gentle and kind person whose cooking was delicious. She was especially good at making *banh canh* soup, a Vietnamese version of Japanese udon but with thicker noodles topped off with fresh ground shrimp. She used to sell her homemade banh canh some years earlier on the main roads to the bus passengers and the locals. Her small portable business had been very successful, she told my mother.

By now, the instinct for survival was as deeply engrained in me as it was in my mother. So when she was away, I began to cook for myself. I ate the things that grew on our land: tomatoes, papayas, bananas, water spinach and tart squash. I seasoned them with tiny hot chilli peppers, coriander, mint, basil and lemongrass, all of which grew in profusion. I picked wild mushrooms, my favourite, to make stir-fries and soups. I caught the small fish and crayfish that lived in our little rivers and grilled them on sticks over an open fire. I picked young coconuts and drank their fresh juice. In fact, I ate better than I had done in Ben Tre, although I still had yet to grow or put on much weight. No one had taught me how to do all of these things. I had learned them by watching my mother and other people around me.

I remember being very muddy all the time that we lived in Huu Dinh. After a while, I gave up on using our shower and bathed naked in the river instead, simply because it was easier. My fear of Thuy Tinh, the water god, was abated by the fact that these rivers were not very deep or fast, and there seemed to be little risk of drowning. Out of modesty, I always bathed at night, even though this was the time when snakes – and ghosts – were out in full force. My fear of snakes is second only to my fear of water, and ghosts run a close third. Naturally, I had to face all of these phobias in the darkness – which itself ranked number four on my list.

But I wasn't alone. The spectacle of a young girl taking a moonlit bath in a river drew what passed for a crowd in Huu Dinh: a young man who was the son of our nearest neighbour, and Hung, my protector. The two of them used to watch me as though I was an exhibit, making comments to each other and teasing me about how small and scrawny I was. Yet, although this may sound perverted or highly inappropriate to Western readers, in fact there was nothing strange about it. This is because it had nothing to do with sex. In our culture, sex is governed by a strict set of social rules and is always conducted, and even discussed, only in private. Besides that, the children of Vietnam bathe outdoors frequently, and adults will often stop to watch these scenes of childish innocence with a wistful smile of remembrance on their faces – nothing more.

In fact, far from being afraid of Hung, when we weren't arguing I had a small crush on him. And, after our initial period of adjustment to each other, we reached an understanding.

Almost as though we were a young married couple, the source of our discontent was – what else? – money. Specifically *my* money, which my mother gave me on her sporadic visits home and with which I was expected to budget until her next unpredictable visit. Hung demanded that I share this money with him. I told him to get lost. It was mine, and I had no intention of sharing it with anyone. There was never very much to begin with, and I had to sustain myself for weeks on it. So, I used this money to buy food only for myself – especially meat.

I could only obtain meat by walking a great distance. First, I had to follow the perpetually muddy path out of the palm forest and into the rice paddies, crossing many a skinny, quaking footbridge over one of our ubiquitous rivers. Then, I took another muddy path – I didn't even bother wearing shoes in those days, and I was always slipping and falling on my bottom, leaving me sore and covered in mud from head to toe – until I finally came to a larger dirt road. This road, in turn, led to the main highway. It was here that I would find the butcher's shop. I was a slow walker, and the journey took me about an hour or more on foot.

The only meat available was pork, and because there was no refrigeration – indeed, there was no electricity anywhere in that region – the meat would simply be sitting outside in the open air, attracting flies. This didn't bother me in the slightest. I would buy a big chunk of it and carry it back home, where I would cook it with herbs, chillies and rice. It may sound unsanitary, but in fact I never got sick – and it was delicious.

At first, Hung stared at me resentfully as I ate my home-cooked dishes, complaining about having to fend for himself. I reminded him that I was a ten-year-old child, not a woman, and therefore it wasn't my responsibility to cook for him or even to share my food. Eventually, however, Hung hit on a money-making scheme of his own. He hired some local workers to harvest the coconuts from our palm trees, and then he sold them on the highway to thirsty travellers. Technically, these coconuts were my mother's property, but Hung was entitled to some form of income in exchange for his presence, and she didn't tell him to stop. Hung would then buy food with the money that he earned, and in this way, we arrived at a working relationship.

Sometimes, if there was a bright moon, I went out frog-hunting with my neighbours. The men would use long thin spears, and as they got one frog after another they would toss them into the basket I carried. I could never bring myself to actually kill the frogs, but I had no trouble eating them – they were lovely stir-fried with lemongrass, tasting just like young chicken. But on one of these expeditions, I became hysterical when a leech bit my right ankle. It wouldn't let go, even though I kept hitting it with a big stick. Finally, the leech dropped off. My ankle was swollen for weeks – not from the leech bite, which is painless and harmless, but from hitting myself. I related this incident to my mother the next time I saw her, but her only reaction was to shrug her shoulders.

'What do you expect when you hit yourself with a stick?' she said.

Enrolling in school was not a requirement for Vietnamese children under the Communists. It was, however, free – all one needed was the will to be educated. This I had in abundance. So, every day I made the walk along those same muddy paths to school, which was in the same central area as the butcher's shop.

The school was an old one-storey building divided into five rooms. In my classroom, there were about ten long wooden tables with chairs, a blackboard and a small desk for the teacher. We had no books. Instead, we copied our lessons from the board into our workbooks, then memorised them. Behind the school was a garden where students worked for Good Citizenship grades and extra credit points. At the end of each quarter, those students who achieved the highest level of garden productivity received the best grades. Usually, the boys were graded higher than the girls, especially if they happened to have relatives in the government. Already, the so-called idealism of the Communists was revealed to me for what it was: just the same old anti-girl nonsense as before, called by a different name. If all workers were equal under Communism, then why did boys still receive preferential treatment? And why should students with Party connections be rewarded more than those with none?

Perhaps I didn't phrase the above questions to myself in quite this way, but I was nonetheless aware that things weren't right, and it only contributed to my unhappiness. I may have been content from time to time in Huu Dinh, but I was never happy.

I had suffered too much already in my short life to have the naturally carefree attitude that all children are born with. Of course, I was not the only child in Vietnam who had experienced tragedy, but I was also suffering from having been raised by parents who were emotionally cold and distant – from each other and from me. I would have had emotional problems even if there had never been any war. Added to all of that, I missed my sister

Hanh terribly. I cried many times at night, in complete darkness and in bed alone. I wished that she were still alive, lying there next to me to keep me company and keep me warm. I was a lonely, lost child.

Because I was a strange, quiet little girl, I did not make any effort to gain new friends at school. Instead, I tended to isolate myself from the other students. To them, because of the clothes I was wearing, I was the new rich girl who came from a bigger village. To my eyes, my clothes were old and simple, but to these small village children, they looked new and fashionable. Despite all that some of them were nice enough to ask me to play games with them. One of the popular girls' games was *choi chuyen* (bamboo jacks) for which you use ten thin, rounded bamboo sticks and a ball, which traditionally is a fig, a miniature variety of eggplant, a small rock or a clod of clay. The player tosses the ball into the air and picks up the sticks on the floor while the ball is still in the air. She must catch the ball before it falls back and touches the floor.

Another fun one was the 'Ooooo' game, where the player has to make it to the other side of the line, which was drawn in dirt in the playground dividing it into two sides, while saying 'Oooo'. If she stopped saying 'Ooooo', the other team would chase her and try to stop her before she could get back to her own side. But if she had touched someone while she was oooing, then that person must be kept prisoner in the back end of her team. Whichever team had no one left to play, lost.

Gradually, though, I became more and more introverted, and all I could think of was my own unhappiness. My insecurity and emotional instability translated into withdrawn or sometimes downright hostile behaviour, and my classmates were quick to pick up on this. I was not well liked. Once, a girl borrowed my pen and then claimed she had lost it in the river, though everyone knew she hadn't – yet no one spoke up in my defence. I had no help from the teachers either, as they seemed to be indifferent. Sometimes, I couldn't work out why they were there – it seemed to me like they were just fulfilling a forced national duty.

After a few months, I developed a crush on a tall, good-looking boy in my class. He seemed to like me back, and for the first time in my life I felt that I might have a real friend. I was overjoyed. He even took me home to meet his parents. They were polite but cool. His father had been with the Viet Cong in the war and he now held an important post in the local government. My own father's loyalties were well known in this small village, and this was perhaps the cause of his attitude towards me. But the people of Vietnam were trying to put the war behind them and get on with life. Maybe the old men sat and talked politics, but we children were only concerned about the present.

So, I had a boyfriend. It was wonderful. We walked and talked and played games together. He told me about his father's time serving in the North Vietnamese forces. He took me around and showed me the daily chores he had to do on the family's land and in their rice fields. Sometimes we held hands and we kissed once or twice on the cheek, but always shyly, chastely, as we were very young.

A year later, however, a new girl arrived in our school, and he promptly fell in love with her. I couldn't believe it and I confronted my boyfriend about it, demanding that he choose between me or her.

'You are a difficult girl to please,' he told me – and dumped me on the spot.

I was heartbroken. I already knew that life was hard. Now, I was beginning to learn that it was dangerous to trust anyone. My attitude got worse and worse. The more I craved affection, attention and respect, the less of it I received, from children and adults alike. For a long time, I felt pain and bitterness whenever I saw people being happy together. I resented the fact that my happiness had been stolen both by the war and by the fact that my family was the way it was. Slowly, I began to close my heart off to everyone.

I don't know for sure what was going on emotionally with my mother then, but I imagine she must have felt much the same as I did, only with the added pressure of having to make a living and of trying to figure out what her place was in this new Communist-run world. On the odd occasions that we saw each other, Mother and I shared hardly anything with each other about our daily lives. For example, I managed to keep my boyfriend and our break-up a secret from her. I did not know if Hung knew about it, but I can't imagine that he would have cared much if he did.

I thought that my mother seemed very cold and didn't care much about me. I was not sure why, but I thought that maybe she wanted to forget about Hanh and somehow I reminded Mother of her beloved dead daughter. I often asked myself if Mother had wished that I had died, too. That way, there would be no one left to remind her of the tragedy.

Occasionally, during Mother's increasingly rare visits home, she would take me to visit Uncle Hieu and his family in their new country home. These trips provided a little bit of fun in an otherwise dark existence. My five cousins – Nhan, Duyen, Thuy, Tam and Oanh – and I used to catch fish together by damming up one of the smaller rivers and trapping whatever happened to be between the banks. Then we would bail out the water, bucket by bucket, until the fish were revealed, flopping madly in the mud. Then they became our dinner.

Like my father, Uncle Hieu was a big drinker. One night, he got drunker than usual but nevertheless insisted on riding all the way home from the village centre on a mobilette. Incredibly, he survived the trip but then lost control of his scooter and sailed into his house, breaking a lot of furniture – and both of his legs. My general opinion of men did not improve after this incident.

My cousins were all expert swimmers. I had yet to conquer my fear of the water god, but with the five of them egging me on, I tried. I drank a lot of river water again. As I doggy-paddled along with my nose just above the surface, I could see pieces of human faeces floating along at eye level. All the rivers around there were used as latrines, as well as for washing dishes, clothes and bodies. I hated swimming in this filth, and I was still terrified of Thuy Tinh, but I made myself do it. I don't truly understand my reasons for being determined to overcome my fears, but it was as if some hidden part of me knew that someday I was going to have to face this spirit down once and for all and show him who was the stronger. I had no idea how a puny little girl such as myself could hope to win such a confrontation. I was just obeying some inner instinct, preparing myself for an unknowable future.

As it turned out, this instinct would very shortly save my life.

Boat People

L ife in Huu Dinh continued in more or less the same fashion for nearly two years. Except for the occasional bus trip to Saigon, which I undertook with Mother, I saw nothing of the world outside my own little village.

As much as I resented being kept away from the hustle and bustle of humanity, far from seeming like reprieves or special events, these visits to the big city frightened me. I had grown accustomed to the peace and quiet of my new surroundings. The only sounds I heard in Huu Dinh were natural ones: birds singing, rivers burbling, wind rustling the leaves of the palm trees. Saigon was full of every kind of noise imaginable, the predominant one being the tinny two-stroke whine of thousands of overworked mobilettes. And the Communists hadn't done anything to improve the buses that were our only mode of transportation to and from the city. They were still the same old death traps they had always been, and I dreaded getting on them, not knowing if I would disembark in Saigon or the afterlife.

One time, Mother took me to see some of her friends in Saigon. When we were in the capital city, we stayed with one of her friends who also employed Mother to make ao dai at her tailoring shop. In the morning, we went out to Ben Thanh market to eat. Mother ordered *bun* for her and for me, *banh hoi*. *Bun thit nuong* is a popular Vietnamese dish made from a combination of grilled pork and vermicelli noodles over a bed of green salad and sliced cucumber, herbs and bean sprouts. It also includes a few chopped-up egg rolls, spring onions and shrimp, and is served with roasted peanuts on top and a small bowl of *nuoc cham* (a prepared Vietnamese fish sauce). Banh hoi is an authentic Vietnamese noodle that is extremely thin and woven into intricate bundles. It is often topped with finely chopped spring onions and a complementary meat dish, served with a small bowl of nuoc cham and broth soup. After breakfast, Mother took me around the market and bought some tropical fruits. I especially liked fresh jackfruit, lychees, longans, rambutan, locally grown mangos, mangosteen, soursop and durian, the last of which can be very off-putting to Westerners because of its very strong smell.

Saigon was a bustling city. There were motor scooters and bicycles running in every direction. I felt like I was seriously risking my life just crossing the street. There were young women wearing ao dai and the famous non la riding bicycles to schools, while whole families would sometimes be clinging on to a tiny mobilette. People were honking, talking and yelling across each other while manoeuvring skilfully among hundreds of scooters. Mother would be busy chatting with her friends, while I felt lost in the middle of chaos. I wanted to go back to my home in the countryside.

I believe that most children don't have a very clear idea of what their parents' lives are really like. It's their own world that seems real to them, while adults move in some kind of mythical world outside of time. This was particularly the case for me, because I saw my mother so rarely. All I knew was that she abandoned me with clocklike regularity, re-appeared for a few days to hand me a couple of *Dong*, then swept out again, off to Saigon on another jewellery-selling trip. Since she never bothered to explain anything to me, my resentment of her only increased. When I asked her when she would next be home, she would hesitate before giving a vague answer, seeming never to notice the tears in my eyes.

What I didn't know was that things were getting tighter and tighter for her all the time. The Communists were making life unpleasant for everyone who had supported the South during the war. Although my mother was by no means a high-ranking political figure or an intellectual – the two groups that suffered the most retribution from the Viet Cong – she was still connected by blood and marriage to the family of Thanh, my wealthy Chinese step-grandfather. As far as the Communists were concerned, Thanh and his family represented capitalism at its worst: they had all grown fat and wealthy from the labour of others. Thanh himself had lost everything in Ben Tre to the Communists, although his other family members, most of whom were now living in Saigon, had managed to hide many of their assets and masqueraded as normal working-class Vietnamese.

While there had been no consequences for her as yet, Mother constantly heard terrifying tales of the things that were being done to other victims of the new regime. She must have dreaded the moment when she would feel a hand on her shoulder and turn around to come face to face with a representative of the People's Office of Supervision and Control – sort of a cross between a Neighbourhood Watch Programme and the KGB.

I think, too, that there must have been other things going on to make life unpleasant for her. I don't know what they were, but no doubt the threat of being sent to a re-education camp was quite real for anyone who wasn't an outright Party loyalist. These camps were about as educational for non-Communists as Auschwitz or Bergen-Belsen were for non-Nazis. To this day, it is not known how many people died in them in the years after the war. But the last of their prisoners was not released until 1992 – and by that time he was nothing more than a broken, brainwashed old man.

Communism knows nothing of tolerance; in every culture where it takes root, the leaders feel it necessary to purge society, always bloodily, of all remnants of the previous regime. It never works, of course, not completely; it only has the effect of terrifying everyone, and causing untold pain and suffering.

But back then, I still knew nothing of politics or of the strange workings of the world of adults. All I knew was that one day in December of 1978 my mother re-appeared in Huu Dinh. She brought Hung and me inside the house, made sure no one else was around and said, 'We're leaving.'

'Leaving Huu Dinh?'

'Leaving Vietnam,' my mother corrected me.

Hung's jaw dropped. So did mine.

'What? When?' I said.

'Tomorrow night.'

'But how?'

'By boat,' my mother said. 'We're sailing across the sea to Malaysia. And then hopefully from there we could be sent to *My* [America] to live with your half-uncles, Trieu and Nghia.'

My heart sank. So Thuy Tinh was to have another shot at me after all!

Mother explained that she had just spent every penny she'd earned selling jewellery to secure us two places on a fishing boat. There was no time to say goodbye to anyone. We were leaving – now. I had about thirty seconds to get ready, and then we were off.

This turn of events came as a total shock. I had little knowledge of the world outside Vietnam. There were nearby countries called Cambodia, Thailand and Laos; I knew, in an abstract sense, about China and Russia. Somewhere out there, America lurked: a giant, powerful beast whose lair was on the other side of the world. But I, like nearly all Vietnamese people, was largely ignorant of what was going on outside my village. We had no access to radio or television news. Even newspapers were hard to come by. We didn't travel. One poorly understood consequence of being a Third-Worlder is the almost total lack of information on any subject whatsoever. This ignorance can ultimately be just as crippling as poverty or disease.

I had never contemplated leaving our country, even when things had been at their worst – mostly because I hadn't even known it was an option. Now, the thought that we could just shed our past as though it were a coat that had grown unfashionable was both tantalising and terrifying.

But poor Hung looked miserable.

'What about me?' he asked. 'Am I going, too?'

'I've only enough money for two places, Hung,' said my mother. 'But to thank you for all you've done for my daughter, I have a present for you. I give you this land and this house for your very own, for ever. It's yours. I will give you the deed right now.'

Hung's face brightened considerably. He had nothing to fear from staying, after all. He was only an uncomplicated country fellow. He would be content to harvest coconuts and sell them to travellers for the rest of his life and would never feel that he lacked for anything. He was the ideal Communist worker – dull, unimaginative and complacent. At that moment, I actually envied Hung. He could predict with almost complete accuracy what every day of the rest of his life would be like. There would be no surprises for him. As for me – who knew what the future would hold? No one, not even my mother, could answer that question.

But one thing was for sure: I knew my immediate future would involve water. And that knowledge filled me with foreboding.

We took nothing with us, not even our legal papers, because there would be no room for luggage and, besides that, we had nothing worth taking anyway. There was no time for farewells. Mother and I made the journey to My Tho, a town not far from Ben Tre, at the mouth of the Mekong – the same river in which I had first confronted the wrath of Thuy Tinh. We didn't get there until it was nearly dark, and I was consumed with anxiety. Would the angry water god remember me and try once again to drag me down? I hoped fervently that he would never even know I was on the boat. Maybe, just maybe, I thought, if I stayed quiet and kept hidden, I would get lucky and escape his wrath once more. And if I succeeded, I would never tempt him again. I would promise to stay out of sight of water for the rest of my life.

We arrived at the collection point, which was a small house on the bank of the river. Inside, there were all kinds of fruit set out on a table. We were told we could take as much as we wanted. I didn't bother – I assumed we were only going to be on the boat for a day or so. But most other people crammed their pockets and bags as full as possible.

Some of the other passengers were already there before us, but others kept arriving long after we did, until it seemed there were hundreds of people milling around in the dusk, bumping into each other and whispering pardons. Silence was imperative. To be caught meant – well, we didn't think about that, but it would have been bad.

Our situation was not as simple as it seemed on the surface. The Communists were actually encouraging people like us to leave the country, because it saved them the trouble and expense of having to re-educate us. So, they would not have been angry with us for the simple act of trying to leave. But they would have had to arrest us anyway, because the flood of boat people from Vietnam was becoming an embarrassment to them. How could they claim to have created a workers' paradise when so many thousands of people would risk death rather than stay? It was blowing their story completely.

And, of course, once we were arrested, we knew we would then have been subjected to the brainwashing that Communists the world over seem to think is such an effective way of converting people to their cause. Some of us would have survived this, but many would have died a month, or a year, or ten years down the road.

It was easier not to get caught in the first place.

I looked around at all the people. The youngest was two months old; the oldest was a grandfather of sixty. There were lots of sick people. I even saw a very pregnant woman who looked like she belonged in bed. My mother's current boyfriend, Nhon, was there with his two sons, who bookended me in age. I had not seen them or talked to them for months, so I hung back while they whispered nervously amongst themselves. I was surrounded by strangers. My year or so in rural isolation hadn't improved my social skills, and

I still had not even begun to process all the losses I had suffered; I had only learned to hide my pain and to protect myself from further damage through withdrawn or hostile behaviour.

Then, I saw a face I hadn't seen for years: Kiet.

Kiet was a boy about my age, and he was one of the few people on earth whom I could call a friend. His mother, Thu Ba, was there, too. Thu Ba and my mother were also close friends. In fact, since Thu Ba was married to one of the sons of my wealthy Chinese step-grandfather, Kiet was sort of a relative of mine – although the connection was tenuous even by Vietnamese standards. But he was a familiar face, and a comforting one. Kiet looked as scared as I felt. We gravitated towards each other immediately.

I had met Kiet many times when his mother invited us to dinner at their home. Aunt Thu Ba was a good cook. I especially liked her *thit cha bong*, or cotton pork meat. Well-cooked pork is crushed then pulled apart. After the meat is shredded, it is transferred to a dry frying pan over low heat until the meat becomes as light as a feather. I loved to eat thit cha bong for breakfast in rice soup or with a bowl of rice for dinner.

Kiet and I used to play with each other in the streets outside their house, which was conveniently located right next door to my Aunt Tuyet's place. During the Tet (New Year), Mother often took me to visit his grandmother, who lived just a mile away, to eat and play cards with all of their relatives. It's traditional in Vietnam for families and friends from far and wide to gather and cook special holiday foods such as *banh chung*, a square cake representing the earth, and *banh day*, a round cake representing the sky. But the best thing was that all of the children received new money, *tien li xi*, from their parents and elders for good luck and prosperity in the coming year, and were free to spend this on gambling games such as *bau cua ca cop* and cards.

'Where have you been?' Kiet whispered. 'I haven't seen you for a long time!'

'I've been out in the country,' I whispered back.

'Do you know where we're going?'

'Quiet!' someone ordered.

We fell silent.

After a moment, Kiet said plaintively, 'I wish my father was here.'

Only then did I remember that Kiet and I had something else in common: we had both lost our fathers during the war. But Kiet's father hadn't died in combat, even though he was in the army. His death had come about in an even more terrible fashion.

One day, while drinking with his friends in a bar, Kiet's father and three other soldiers had decided to play a betting game that Westerners call Russian Roulette. In this game, the participants make their bets, then take turns putting a gun to their own heads and pulling the trigger. The gun is a six-shot revolver, and it's loaded with only one bullet, so there is a one-in-six chance of dying. Add another round, and the odds change to two-in-six, at which point the betting goes up accordingly. This is the game that was featured in the 1978 film *The Deerhunter*, starring Robert DeNiro and Meryl Streep. It's inconceivable to most of us to risk throwing our lives away in such a careless way, but I believe that the popularity of this game in those days showed how little human life was valued during the war, and it was also an indication of the despair that the soldiers must have felt, knowing they were probably going to die violently anyway. The potential for profit was large, too. A soldier risking his life at a betting table for half an hour could make as much as he did risking it in the jungle for a whole year. But Kiet's father's luck ran out.

Like my mother, Thu Ba was very pretty. She'd had a little more luck with men than my mother had, as she'd remarried and at the end of the war she gave birth to a baby girl. But her second husband had been killed in the fighting, and then her new baby died from one of the virulent illnesses that claimed the lives of so many children in our country. No one in Vietnam was spared the kind of tragedy that most Westerners only read about in newspapers.

Of course, we were glad to be fleeing poverty and persecution. But we were also leaving behind our hearts. I wonder now, as a mother myself, what my mother and Thu Ba really could have been feeling as they turned their backs on their ancestral homeland – where they had buried their parents, husbands and children, as well as countless generations of ancestors – and faced a future full of uncertainty. It was too dark for me to be able to see their facial expressions; I could not tell if they were frightened or sad. As for me, I did not know what to think.

When darkness fell, the men in charge of the boat gave us the signal, and we all walked down to the riverbank. There was something eerie, and not a little poignant, about the sound of hundreds of feet trying and failing to be quiet. There were fruit trees everywhere, and the velvet air was redolent with their perfume. We began to board the boat. The atmosphere was charged with tension and fear. Although total silence was insisted upon, small children were crying, and I'm sure not a few adults were, too. We were not the first boat people to leave Vietnam. Many, many thousands had gone before us, and the tales of the perils they faced on their journeys had come back to the ears of those they left at home. Those who knew what we were in for were crying the most, I'm sure. Those who knew nothing, like me, thought it was just some big adventure.

The boat itself was just a simple fishing craft, scarcely big enough to hold fifty people. Yet there were 350 of us on board. Mother and I were crammed down into the hold, along with as many others as they could fit down there. We lost sight of Kiet and his mother from here. Inside, it was unbearably hot, and there was no air. Also, it stank of rotting fish. Before long, Mother lost patience. She grabbed me by the hand and pulled me through the cemented mass of humanity up to the deck, ignoring the whispered complaints and protests of those she had to elbow out of her way. This was most un-Vietnamese behaviour, but it was also typical of Mother, whose first instinct was always to survive. She pulled us forward until we were next to the captain's cabin. There she claimed us a tiny spot of deck, where at least we could get a breath of fresh air. We could see an ailing glimmer of light coming from the wheelhouse, but there was no other source of illumination anywhere. Even the stars had been blotted out by clouds. The fishermen had logically chosen a moonless night to make this run. It was so dark I couldn't even see my hand in front of my face.

We cleared the mouth of the Mekong, not a sound coming from our ship except that of whimpering children and whispered prayers. Everyone, it seemed, was keeping that rickety boat afloat through sheer willpower, praying to all the gods they could think of – including, most likely, Thuy Tinh. Mother and I did not pray, at least not consciously. We simply sat, numb and silent, waiting for whatever would happen next.

It was December, the most turbulent month on the South China Sea. By the time we cleared the river's mouth and headed out into the open sea, the water had grown considerably rougher. There was a running swell that seemed massive to me – at least two or three feet. I was not able to sleep at all. When I closed my eyes, all I could hear was the sound of water, and this creepy noise frightened me. The wet sea air was cold at night and made me shiver. When the sun came up, I realised, to my horror, that the water was less than two feet from the deck's surface. I could have reached out and touched it – though I didn't dare for fear that Thuy Tinh would grab me and pull me under.

With the increasing waves, people began to get seasick. It was likely that none of the people on board our boat had ever been to sea before. Many were vomiting, and most of them didn't make it to the side first. The deck was slick with it; it was smeared on people's faces and clothing, and it smelled awful.

I closed my eyes and pretended I was somewhere else. I saw that I was walking on a white sandy beach in Vung Tau, a famous beach resort in Vietnam. Even though I had never been to the city myself, I had heard Mother talking about it. She might have been there with her friends in Saigon. Then I pretended that I was reading the kung-fu books and the hero characters were there in front of me like I was watching a live film in a cinema. My eyes slowly closed . . .

During that first day, it became apparent that we were badly overloaded and that our boat would be swamped by the first really large wave that hit it. The decision was made to throw half our food and water overboard. There was no other choice. Some people protested, but they were overruled, and jugs of water and dozens of pounds of food were tossed into the sea. But this did little to help our boat, which continued to labour along like a pack mule carrying a football team, scarcely making any progress through the water.

The second day and the third night passed in this way as well – only now people were hungry and thirsty. Fights over the remaining food and water began to break out all over the boat. In retrospect, I realise now that this fighting was yet another frightening aspect of our journey. Vietnamese society has always placed the utmost importance on good behaviour and respect for one's parents and elders. Now, after only two days at sea, the entire social structure that we had all been born into was breaking down in a way that none of us had ever seen before. Young adults pushed old people out of the way to get at what they wanted; adults stole food and water from children. This only served to enhance our feelings of fragility and vulnerability. Was everything we had known in our lives nothing more than a dream, no more substantial than a wisp of fog? Did our lives matter in the slightest?

The answer to this last question was becoming increasingly clear.

Mother and I sat, unmoving, with our backs against the windows of the captain's cabin, trying to ignore the chaos around us, as well as the beating sun and the strong breeze. At night, we slept in the same sitting positions, braving the chilly winds of the ocean. We were like two garden statues exposed to the elements, and we tried to have no more emotion than statues would, either.

'Mother, who is the captain?' I asked weakly.

'He is a fisherman,' Mother whispered.

'How do you know him?' I asked, looking at her curiously.

'A good friend in Saigon connected us,' she explained.

'Do you think that we will find land soon?' I enquired.

'Let's hope so, OK? Now sleep,' Mother sharply cut off the conversation.

That third night, mercifully, it rained. We were now wet and cold, but at least we could drink enough rain to keep us alive. Were it not for that rain, I think I would have died on that boat.

At night, when I looked out over the ocean, all I saw was total darkness. During the day, there was nothing but water. Water everywhere. There was nothing attractive or romantic about it. The clear-blue cloudless sky above seemed as vast as the sea below, and this hugeness only added to the feeling that we were like an insignificant group of bugs bobbing on a cork. It would make no difference to the world if we were swept under by the next wave, and no one would ever know what had happened to us.

The waves were so big now that I was terrified each one would be the one that would knock us over. They pounded ceaselessly against the hull of the boat, day and night. It was the most frightening sound I had ever heard, even more so than the bombs or missiles of my early childhood. Each wave was like a rocket attack all of its own, yet they kept coming, hundreds of them, thousands, tens of thousands. I was trapped in a black hole of fear and despair.

By the third day, we were out of food and water completely. People prayed, cried, pleaded with deities and ghosts. The sound of wailing children filled the air.

In addition to fear, I was now consumed by a thirst like nothing I had ever known before. All my life, I had taken pains to avoid water. Now I wished for nothing else. I thought of the rivers back in Huu Dinh: how casually I had skipped across our little palm-tree bridge without ever once stopping to appreciate the wealth of liquid trickling along below, free for the taking. I would even have given anything to be back doggy-paddling in my uncle Hieu's muddy river. Never mind the filth. I would open my mouth and drink deeply.

I began to grow delirious. It was maddening to be surrounded by so much water and not be able to drink any of it. I got up and began to hunt around blindly for something, anything that would offer me some moisture. Once, I spied a mango, but when I grabbed it, a grown man slapped me across the face as hard as he could and snatched it back. Crying, I ran back to my mother to tell her what had happened. But there was nothing she could do about it. She only told me to save my tears, because I would dry up even faster without them.

Severe dehydration stalked the boat like the Grim Reaper. If we did not get more water soon, people would start to die. The little children were all screaming now, a ceaseless, pitiful cacophony of misery. Their voices were hoarse, but still they cried, not knowing when their agony was going to end. The nursing mothers on board were too dehydrated to make any milk for their babies. I had not seen Kiet or Thu Ba since the journey started, even though they were probably just a few feet below us, trapped in the double hell of the airless fish hold. I could not even imagine what it was like down there. And despite my mother's warning, I was unable to stop crying myself. Tears dripped down the back of my throat, mingling with the salt spray that I couldn't help swallowing from time to time.

Once, I made my way to the back of the boat to use the latrine. This was something like a portaloo that one might see on construction sites, except it was simply lashed to the back of the boat, with the bottom open to the sea. Despite this, it still smelled horrific, and I tried not to breathe while I was using it. I felt like I had to pee, and I could even feel the pressure on my bladder, but, try as I might, nothing came. I was so dehydrated that I couldn't even produce enough urine to flush out my kidneys. Weakly, I went back to my mother and collapsed, feeling more dead than alive.

That night, our fourth at sea, we saw a light in the distance – a ship. Everyone began making noise, yelling, blowing horns, banging things together. The light drifted closer, then further away. We never saw what kind of ship it was. No doubt they heard and saw us, but once they realised how many of us there were, they must have decided it was easier just to continue on their way and leave us to our fate.

The next day, the pregnant woman began vomiting. There were no doctors on board, not that it would have mattered if there had been. We didn't even have any water left to give her. She got sicker and sicker throughout the day, then in the afternoon, she died.

There was no discussion. Some men simply grabbed her by the ankles and wrists and tossed her overboard. I watched as her face and rounded belly slowly slipped beneath the surface of the waves. This, for me now when I think back, became the new symbol of being Vietnamese – wasted fertility, losing not just life itself but even the ability to make more life.

We were damned.

Later that day, we saw a dot on the horizon. Over the course of several hours, it came closer to us, until we saw that it was a very big ship – a navy ship. I did not know what country it was from and still don't, but I don't think it was American. It couldn't come any closer for fear of swamping our craft. We waited for them to lower boats and come to our rescue. Everyone was waving, yelling and crying. After a couple of hours of this, during which time the captain of the ship was no doubt waiting for orders about what to do with us, the ship slowly turned and headed back the way it had come. We had been abandoned to die.

That night, everyone who had any tears left cried them all.

The next day, as we came closer to Thailand, there was something new to worry about: pirates. All of us had heard stories of merciless Thai sea bandits attacking ships just like ours, raping the women and girls, stealing everything of value and killing indiscriminately before setting fire to the boat. This very fate had befallen two uncles of mine who left Vietnam in 1977. The pirates succeeded in raping some of the women and in killing some of the men. But my uncles had managed to wrestle a gun away from the pirates and killed one of them instead. Being cowards, like all criminals, the rest fled.

That course of action was very risky, and the men on our boat were too weak with hunger and thirst to take anyone on. Yet they made plans for what they would do if we were attacked. The women on the boat began to darken their faces with black stuff to make themselves look ugly. They also put on clothes to disguise themselves as men.

For another day, we sat and waited, hardly moving.

Eventually, we saw another dark spot on the horizon. It was another navy ship, with a different flag this time. Again, it steamed up as close to us as it dared, but this time they lowered a boat and came towards us. The officer aboard began asking questions in English, of which I understood not one word. Some other people on board did, however, and they explained what was going on. Then the navy men began handing us bottles of water and boxes of food. Sighs and cries of relief and gratitude rose above the sound of the waves. The sailors refused to take anyone with them, however, which made me miserable all over again – at that point, all I or anyone else wanted was deliverance from our floating hell. They were on some sort of mission, and they had no time for us. But we were lucky they had stopped at all. No doubt they saved all our lives.

Another night, another day, another night. Dolphins raced alongside our boat, a sight which once would have thrilled me but now brought me no joy whatsoever. We saw flying fish, then birds. Some of the men began to say that we were getting close to land. I didn't care. I had made up my mind that I would no longer wish for anything ever again. That way, I would never be disappointed.

But, on the seventh day, a strange mass appeared where the sea met the sky. Someone began shouting, 'Land! Land! Land!'

I sat up and looked. Suddenly, all my fears vanished. I no longer dreaded the waves or the pirates. For the first time in a week, I had reason to hope we might survive this journey.

We had sighted Malaysia. We were almost safe.

It was sunset. The sight of that softly glowing celestial orb dipping below the palm trees and the surf hushing gently on white sand beaches seemed to me the most beautiful thing in the world. When we were close enough to shore for small boats to come to us, we dropped anchor. Then we watched as some men came out on the beach and began waving their arms.

But they were not waving us in. They were telling us to go away.

'What are they saying?' I asked my mother.

'They don't want us,' she said, in a tone of disbelief.

Some more men came out on the beach, carrying what looked at that distance like long sticks. They held these sticks up to their shoulders. Suddenly I saw puffs of smoke and heard gunfire.

'They're shooting at us!' I said.

'Stay calm,' said the captain to everyone. 'We're out of range. They can't hurt us.'

So we all sat there like ducks at a carnival, waiting to be popped off. Nobody was hit, and eventually the men on the beach went away.

'Can't we get off now?' I asked.

But we couldn't. We had to wait another night on the ship, with land so close that we could smell it and taste it. Some people wanted to swim to shore, but they were afraid of the water and of the men who had been shooting at us. Nobody knew exactly who they were, but it was obvious we weren't welcome. We would have to wait for someone official to come and tell us what to do.

Night fell, and the wind began to pick up. At first, it seemed like just another hard breeze. But the wind got stronger and stronger, and the waves bigger and bigger, until they were ten feet high and more. Our boat was yanked from side to side as it rode at anchor. One could hear the creaking and groaning of the timbers, and the deck was swamped repeatedly. It became increasingly clear with every battering the fishing boat received that it was not going to survive the storm.

My mother thought fast and ran to the railing, where there was a life preserver. She grabbed it and ran back to me.

'Hurry,' she said. 'Come with me.'

I stood up without objection and followed her to the railing.

'Grab tight,' she said. She put her arms around me.

I looked up into her face, and she down into mine. It was hardly the time for dramatic speeches. With the wind howling, the waves crashing and the boat tossing madly, it was all we could do to keep our feet for those few seconds. Yet I have an image of my mother's face etched into my mind that I will carry with me for ever. Her expression said to me that she had done all she could do in this life to make sure that I was safe. She was telling me, in no uncertain terms, that by jumping off that ship and into the teeth of the storm, we were commending ourselves to whatever capricious forces rule this suffering earth. She had lost every single person and thing that she had ever cared about in the world – except me. Yet she was still not going to just lie down and die. She was going to fight until she had nothing left.

I had never felt particularly loved by my mother up to that point, never felt in any way special or valued. But I realised then, as I realise all the more clearly now, that the only real gift my mother had to give me was that which she had already given me once at birth; then again, every time she had run from the Viet Cong, clutching my infant self to her breast; then again, when she let our father chase her into the streets, instead of allowing him to terrorise her in front of us and put us in danger; yet again when we moved, first to Half-Uncle Hong's then to Huu Dinh; and finally now, when she had traded every last thing she owned for one last shot at survival. She was giving me life. She had nothing else to offer. Now, we were just gambling.

From the very moment of my birth, every moment of our lives had been a fight for survival. Telling me she loved me was pointless. Instead, my mother told me the only thing that made any sense to say to me, her only surviving child: 'Jump.'

And so, we jumped.

I felt nothing when we hit the water – no fear at all. I did not even feel wet. I went down, down into Thuy Tinh's realm. I wasn't even afraid of him any more. If I had seen the angry water god himself striding along the ocean floor, eyes blazing coldly, hands outstretched for my throat, I would not have flinched. I had accepted that it was all over.

Then I opened my eyes. I had not obeyed my mother; I had let go of the life preserver. The boat was still floating, but it was high above me now. There was some moonlight, and the water was churned into phosphorescence as millions of tiny, glowing sea creatures were agitated by the storm. I could see everything clearly. I saw the boat break up directly overhead, as the final wave slammed into it and tore it to shreds. A huge beam with a giant nail protruding from it nearly struck me on its way to the bottom, but I didn't even bother dodging it. I saw the flailing limbs of people as they struggled to swim for shore, and felt nothing for them, no sadness or pity. If this was life, then I wanted nothing to do with it any more. I couldn't even feel sorry for those who were about to pass into the spirit world. After all, that was where we would all end up someday anyway. This futile struggle to remain alive seemed pointless and exhausting. Eleven years had been enough to teach me that nothing was real except loss, suffering and pain. I decided that eleven years of the same lesson over and over was probably enough. I was ready to die.

Then, a mighty force grabbed me, picked me up and pushed me towards shore. At the time, I had no idea what that force was, but now, of course, I know it was a wave, for we had been close enough to shore that we were caught up in the surf – even though the gradual incline of the sea floor here meant that the surf ran up for a long way before finally hitting the beach. But still, it felt like some kind of divine hand, plucking me out of the jaws of death yet again.

Over and over I tumbled, as helpless as a tiny crab. Then, suddenly, I was crawling out of the surf and up onto land. A pair of hands – I never knew whose – grabbed me and pulled me the rest of the way out of the water. I lay there for a long time, half-conscious, trying to work the seawater out of my lungs. So, I reflected calmly, I was to live still more of this life. Again, the news was neither welcome nor unwelcome. I was now just a passenger, staring idly out of the window as events passed me by. Nothing mattered. Nothing.

When I was able, I sat up. I saw a dark form struggling feebly nearby. I could tell that this person was an adult, and so I got up and went over to them. To my astonishment, I saw that it was Mother. Instantly I lost my dispassionate feelings and became hysterical with joy and relief. We held each other and sobbed for a long time, sensing the strangeness of the unmoving land underneath us, not caring that we were being drenched by the storm and the waves. It's a strange fact of human existence that we cling to life in such precarious moments, when giving up would be so much easier. Moments earlier, I had been ready for it all to end. Now, I could hardly contain my happiness at finding myself still breathing.

Another form appeared in the surf. It was a man. He crawled up on his hands and knees, then got to his feet, looked down and saw that he had lost his trousers. Even in that moment, the Vietnamese sense of modesty prevailed. He pulled his sweatshirt down around his knees to hide his nakedness. Then he limped further up the beach and sat down on the sand a little bit away from us.

Occasionally, another person would appear out of the surf. We could see things floating out among the waves, and we knew that there were people struggling for their lives out there, but there was nothing we could do. We stayed in that place all night, not feeling the storm. We were both thinking the same thing: if this storm had struck twenty-four hours earlier, not a single one of us would have survived. We would all have been shark food.

After some time, we saw headlights and heard engines on the other side of the trees. Some men in strange uniforms appeared. They looked Asian, but they were speaking English. Someone among us who could understand them explained what had happened. The men told us to get into the backs of the trucks that were parked on the other side of the trees. We struggled to our feet and did as we were told. Perhaps, I thought, we were going to a re-education camp; perhaps they were taking us somewhere to be killed. We were throwaway people now, without a nation to call our own. Anything could happen to us, and no one would ever know about it.

The trucks did take us to a camp, but no one was shouting at us and no one threatened to kill us. Instead, they simply asked us to get out of the trucks and sit in a group so they could count us.

When all the survivors were together again, the head count was 150. No one could believe it. There had been more than twice that number when we set out from the little village on the Mekong a week earlier. Two hundred souls had been lost in the shipwreck.

When we realised this, we all began to cry. Of all the families that had been on board the ship, hardly a single one remained intact. Small children cried out for their parents and received no answer; parents grabbed children that they thought were theirs, only to find that they were not. Spouses looked frantically for each other among the other worn and haggard faces, to no avail. There had been a family of five, a mother, father and three children, whom my mother knew well. The parents had survived, but all three of the children were gone.

It seemed that everyone except us had lost someone. Later, we would learn that a great number of people on board had been carrying their life savings, which they had converted to gold before leaving Vietnam. Unable or unwilling to let go of it, they had sunk to the bottom instead. It was ironic that so many of those who died were those who were most attached to their earthly possessions, while those of us with practically nothing left to bind us to this life were still stuck in it, with no more to call our own than we had on the day we were born.

In every sense, we were starting over. We were being born again. I could only hope that this time around, fate would be kinder to me. I didn't think I could take much more.

6

Life in the Refugee Camp

For days afterwards, the Malaysian authorities were pulling bodies out of the surf. Many of them had been pounded to a pulp by the storm; others were missing limbs or large chunks of their torsos where sharks had got at them. And many bodies were simply never found.

But Mother and I had survived, again beating the odds. Now our situation had changed drastically for the fourth or fifth time in my life. Instead of being free but living in terror, we were safe, secure – and fenced in by barbed wire, without any of the comforts of home.

In other words, we were in a refugee camp.

Refugees occupy a strange place in the world. They are not guilty of any crime, yet they are not masters of their own freedom. They are completely reliant on the goodwill of strangers. Without this, they are not going anywhere, and they may even die. Sometimes people can spend decades in these camps. There are Palestinian refugee camps in the Middle East that have been in existence for three generations now. No one, not even other Arab countries, will take these people in – despite the fact that all Arabs claim to be brothers. It is impossible for the rest of us to fathom the kind of helplessness and rage that this fosters among the detainees, but I had a taste of it in Malaysia.

By the time we arrived at the camp, there were already 2,500 to 3,000 people living there, and more were arriving every day. We were in such a daze that I scarcely took note of my surroundings. It was so crowded that there was not even enough space for my mother and I to sleep under a roof. We were given a couple of cots side by side in a sea of other cots. The Vietnamese character being what it is, the whole scene was like a very polite and well-ordered version of total insanity. Everyone was in the same state of shock, but we all worked hard at maintaining the standards of behaviour we were used to. In this respect, at least, things had returned to normal. I was grateful for this; I hoped that I would never again be faced with the kind of chaos I had witnessed on the boat.

Those first few days, I slept a lot and drank a lot of water. There was no medical care available. At the time, this didn't bother me, but I know now that I was lucky not to have suffered more serious effects from my spell of dehydration – it can often take as long as a month for the body to recover its natural balance of electrolytes and fluids.

The climate in this part of Malaysia – I had no idea exactly where we were and to this day still do not – was not dissimilar to where we had come from. We were close to both the mountains and the sea, but the temperature and weather were much the same. When it rained, we simply got wet. Once again, we were completely exposed to the elements, always soaked through and always tired from lack of proper sleep.

My mother's boyfriend, Nhon, and his two sons, Toai and Nguyen, had survived the shipwreck. So, to my great delight, had Kiet and Thu Ba. But we were all in shock for weeks; only gradually did we begin to accept the fact that we were getting another chance at life and that we would all have to start over. I had no mirror in which to see myself, but I imagine my expression must have been similar to the stunned looks on the faces of my friends.

Try to pretend, just for a moment, that everything you ever accumulated in your life has been taken away from you and that you have been picked up and set down in an entirely new place, where there is just enough food, clothing and shelter to keep you alive, but no more. Now try to make yourself happy and excited about your condition. This is the plight of the refugee. It's a strange paradox, because we really were lucky to be in that camp, and we were not ungrateful. But there was a strong sense of loss, coupled with the feeling that our lives were on hold until someone agreed to take us in.

Despite our sense of displacement, we settled quickly into a new routine. On Mondays, the head person from each family went to the front courtyard of the camp and stood in line to receive that week's rations. Usually, this consisted of rice and canned sardines. We were grateful for anything at all, but it required a great deal of creativity to prevent such fare from growing monotonous. Some people were better at this than others. People even began to trade rice-and-sardine recipes, and there sprang up a kind of good-hearted competition to see who could prepare them in the most original way.

Soon, some children from the nearby village figured out that we would buy produce from them. A black market developed that traded largely in vegetables and legumes. It was a child-run operation, because we drew less attention to ourselves. We would give the Malaysian children money through the fence, and they would throw the goods over to our side. The authorities in charge of the camp, who were neither friendly nor hostile to us, didn't seem to care too much. Their main concern, since they were Muslims, was that we did not attempt to buy or eat any pork. Pork, of course, is a mainstay of the traditional Vietnamese diet. There were many of us who would have paid any amount for a nice bowl of stir-fried pork and rice. But we couldn't offend our hosts, and, besides that, there probably wasn't a pig for miles around anyway.

Cooking was done on improvised stoves that consisted of three or four large rocks with a space between them large enough to build a fire. For fuel, we scavenged wood from the surrounding countryside. The authorities provided us with a few basic cooking utensils and chopsticks, but they were in no way prepared to deal with the number of refugees coming at them every day. So, beyond these basics, we were on our own.

There was plenty of water, but we had to walk a long way out to a remote well, pump it by hand and carry it back in buckets. The water was muddy, and we had to let it sit for two or three hours before it was drinkable. Of course, water like this was full of bacteria, and it made everyone sick. But it was still better than dying of dehydration on the deck of a ship.

Sanitation, or rather the lack of it, was a big problem in other ways. We had no soap to wash our pots and pans, for example. Nguyen, Nhon's youngest boy, developed a bad case of parasites: one day while using the latrine, he realised there were long, white worms coming out of his rectum. With no medication available, not even the raw material for folk remedies, he just had to learn to live with them.

Our latrines were four large holes in the ground, and they were not far enough from the camp. When the wind blew in our direction, the smell was unbearable. The sheer number of flies turned the piles of human waste from yellow to black. We all became very good at holding our breath for long periods of time while squatting over the pits. But there was nothing to prevent people from accidentally toppling over into them, and it happened often enough that it was a problem. With nothing to clean themselves with except muddy water, those who were unfortunate enough to take such a tumble into the pits would stay smelly for days, sometimes weeks.

And then there was the boredom. I spent most of my spare time watching old men play Chinese chess. My old flair for self-teaching shone through again, and soon I had mastered the rules and was able to play along with them.

My mother, too, was slowly piecing together whatever jagged puzzle-pieces of normality she could gather. She began, once again, to sew ao dai for the ladies. Most of her clients usually wrote to relatives who had already made it to other countries, asking them to send them the material, because many of them had nothing much to wear. From start to finish, each garment took Mother exactly a month to complete. With the money she earned from this – incredibly, some people had managed to hang onto their gold through the storm, while others were getting money sent to them from relatives in other parts of the world – she began to take English lessons.

Her teacher was a Vietnamese man named Nguyen Ngoc Ngan. He had been on the same boat as us and had lost his wife and child in the shipwreck. But still he tried to help other people, to contribute something to the community, and for this I remember him with admiration. This man spoke very good English, and he had many students, because there were a lot of people anxious to make their way to America, Canada or other English-speaking countries. Many years later, Nguyen Ngoc Ngan was to become a well-known writer in North American expatriate Vietnamese communities. He wrote both fiction and non-fiction, and some of his work, which is in Vietnamese, dealt with the shipwreck and life in our camp.

When I wasn't playing chess with the old men, I tried to spend time with my friends – except by this time, after all I had been through, I simply wasn't able to have normal friendships with other children. I shouldn't wonder to learn now that all the children in the camp were going through the same emotional turmoil as I was, but of course I was aware only of my own problems, and I thought I was the only one who was suffering. Nguyen was a gentle and shy boy, but Toai was a rebel, like me. We used to fight with each other constantly, and Kiet and I fought about as often as we got along. Sometimes we played hide and seek around the camp. Other times we went into the community kitchen to watch other people cooking. Other than that, we just sat around doing nothing. Life in the camp was boring and dull.

My mother despaired of my behaviour. Instead of being grateful for my life, I was resentful of every little thing that didn't go my way. To her, it seemed like I was always jealous of everyone and always wanting more. Of course, my problems ran much deeper than that. But no one could see that at the time; or rather, no one was in a position to do anything about it. Everyone was grappling with the same losses. There were no group therapy sessions, no self-help television programmes, no guidance counsellors or psychotherapists or anti-depressants. We just had to keep on going . . . somehow.

After three months in this place, Mother and I were finally moved to a spot under a roof. This was like going from a cardboard box on the street to the penthouse of the Hilton. Finally, we were protected from the weather.

Around the same time, there arrived delegations of people from the USA, Canada, France, Australia, the United Kingdom, Italy, Spain and Germany – all the countries that had agreed to accept some of us boat people. These delegations came to conduct interviews to determine our status and to see whether we were eligible for immigration. Mother was determined to make it to America no matter what – she already had two half-brothers in California, the same ones who had managed to fight off the pirate attack. I knew that with Mother on the case, we would get there eventually, even if we had to swim.

When our turn came to be interviewed, Mother and I were prepared to have to struggle to make ourselves understood, but we were highly impressed when the members of the delegation began asking us questions in Vietnamese. They wanted to know where all our documents were. At the bottom of the South China Sea, we said. Mother told them about our losses in the war, the journey across the sea, the shipwreck. I could see in their faces that they were moved by our story. Then they told us that my father's service in the Army of the Republic of Vietnam meant that we were eligible for political refugee status – which meant we had a chance to move to the States. We were elated. But we would have to wait, we were told. Every month, they would post a new list with the names of those who would be allowed to come. We should keep checking that list, they said, until we saw our names.

I was thrilled by the thought of America. Mother had told me that if we could make it to America she would be able to find a job and make some money so that we could have a house and a car, and I would be able to go back to school. We would be free to live wherever we wanted and to travel without fear of being arrested. She also said that we might be living with my uncles, who would help us and support us while we got settled, which was a great relief for both of us.

I was so excited by all of this that I began running to the bulletin board every day. I had such high hopes that every time our names failed to appear, I would run back to my mother, crying. But after three months of disappointment, I couldn't take it any more. I stopped going to check. And that, of course, was when our names appeared.

'Go to the board,' someone told us. 'I think you've been accepted!'

So Mother and I ran, in a frenzy of excitement.

The person hadn't been mistaken. There we were: Nguyen Suong, Nguyen Dung.

We were going to America.

We had arrived in the camp in December of 1978. In July of 1979, we bade farewell to the place that had been our home for seven months. There was a row of five buses waiting to take us to the airport. We waited patiently until they called our names, though we were terrified that a mistake had been made and that our names would not be called after all; that we would have to go back inside and stay in the camp for ever.

But this didn't happen. They did call us, and as we mounted the steps of the bus and took our seats, I felt as though I was being carried up high by Son Tinh, the god who defeated Thuy Tinh by causing the mountains to rise underneath him. I turned once and waved to the mournful faces watching us from inside the gates. Nhon, his sons, Thu Ba and Kiet were still behind the fence. No one had volunteered to take them yet.

Mother and I had had nothing to pack when we left the camp. We were wearing clothes that had come out of aid boxes. We had been allowed to choose two outfits each, plus a pair of shoes. Still, this was more than we had arrived with. As the buses pulled away, we saw for the first time what kind of place we had been in. The camp was in a remote area of Malaysia, far from any towns or cities. The roads were rough and unpaved. When we stopped for lunch at a roadside stand, we saw our first locals – not counting the guards at the camp – and I was shocked to see them eat their food with their fingers, as though they were little better than cavemen. To Vietnamese people, who always use chopsticks, this seemed very bad manners.

We arrived at the airport in Kuala Lumpur after a bus journey of several hours. There, we were met by some American officials. These people handed us oversized plastic bags containing our new identity documents. These were what would allow us to live in the US, and I clung to that bag tighter than I had to the life preserver my mother had handed me as we jumped off the fishing boat. I could not even imagine what new hell I would be plunged into if I lost it.

Then we boarded the aeroplane – the first of my life, of course. I remember that when we were asked by the flight attendants what we would like to drink, Mother wanted some Coke, but she did not know how to say it in English, so we ended up drinking plain water. And from this point on, my memory is a blank. I was either extremely exhausted and fell asleep or my poor little Vietnamese village girl's mind was so overloaded that it simply shut down when faced with the concept of flying over the ocean to the fabled land of America. It did not seem possible that such a thing was happening to me.

I didn't know it yet, but I had already ceased to be Dung and was slowly turning into Juliet. It was a transformation that would not be completed for many years, and it would be a painful process.

We thought that things would be easier for us now that we were going to be Americans. America was a perfect place, where the streets were paved with gold and everyone was wealthy.

How wrong we were. In so many ways, getting on that boat in My Tho had been the start of a journey that would not end for decades. Once you leave home, you never really belong anywhere else. You may come to roost in one place for years, but you are still a refugee, still on the run. Certainly, we were lucky beyond belief to be going to the States. But if we thought that everything was going to be fine from now on, we couldn't have been more mistaken.

The next thing I remember is landing in San Francisco. And thus began the newest and strangest chapter of my life so far.

Part 2

America, 1979–96

7

America: The Beginning

It was mid-July of 1979 when Mother and I landed in San Francisco. The plane arrived behind schedule, so it was too late to catch our connecting flight to Los Angeles. Somehow, with our near-total lack of English, we made our predicament known to those in charge, and we ended up staying the night in a two-star hotel near the airport.

I have friends now who would turn their noses up at two stars, but up to that point in my life I had never even taken a bath in a real bathtub with running water. Less than forty-eight hours earlier, Mother and I had considered a shelter with a thatched roof and no walls to be the pinnacle of luxury. Now, I found myself in a room with a colour television, a bathroom equipped with toilet, tub and sink, and two of the softest beds on earth. We ate beefsteaks with French fries for dinner and Mother ordered Coke to drink by pointing at the photo on the menu. It was definitely the best meal I had ever eaten, and we were fortunate that the humanitarian government aid programme was paying for all of our travel and accommodation expenses.

We would have been content to stay in that hotel room for the rest of our lives. The beds enveloped us so completely that we slept late, nearly missing our connecting flight again, so we didn't have time to eat any breakfast. Also, there was no room in our tiny stomachs for it; we were still too full from dinner the night before.

In the hotel lobby, we managed to find a Vietnamese man who was also going to Los Angeles. True to form, Mother instantly adopted him as our temporary male authority figure. We got onto the right aeroplane with his assistance, then made the two-hour flight to LA. After disembarking, we had to go through some kind of passport control. Then we emerged into a waiting area, which was a sea of strange faces of all shapes and colours. There were more different kinds of people in that one place than I had even known existed.

The plan had been for my mother's half-brothers to meet us. The arrangement had been made by the US immigration service several weeks before our arrival, so, of course, they had been expecting us the day before. Having waited fruitlessly for hours, they'd gone home again to await a phone call from someone who knew what was going on. Naturally, Mother and I knew nothing about this; all we knew was that they weren't there to meet us. Our unspoken fear was that they had changed their minds about letting us live with them. It would have been perfectly within their rights to do so, but the prospect of having to fend for ourselves in such a strange place was terrifying. Los Angeles seemed like a huge city – and we hadn't even made it out of the airport yet. To say we were scared is an understatement. I even caught myself wishing, once or twice, for the familiarity of the refugee camp.

There we were – two tiny Vietnamese females, with no luggage except our oversized plastic bags that had the word IMMIGRATION printed on them in bright blue ink. They might as well have said VICTIMS – PLEASE ROB US. Not that we had anything to steal, of course. Luckily, our protector on the connecting flight noticed our predicament, and he offered to take us home to stay with his family until my uncles could be located. Mother lost no time in accepting his offer, and soon we were on our way.

On the way from the airport, I was in awe. I had never seen so many cars in my life, and the freeways had so many lanes. I wondered how our new friend knew which one to drive in. As I looked out of the window and then round to the back of the car, the freeway looked like two long fat snakes crawling side by side.

I couldn't understand any of the road signs and eventually I fell asleep – perhaps the snakes and the signs had hypnotised me.

I don't remember the name of this man who helped us, but I will never forget his house as long as I live. It was the first American home I was ever in, and it exceeded my expectations many times over. Much more luxurious than the hotel room, it had yet another feature I had never seen before – a thick, white shag carpet. It looked as expensive and spotless as a ceremonial gown. Particularly because it was white, I was reluctant to walk on it. Just the sight of it made me feel like a dirty refugee child who didn't belong in this place called America.

But the man's family were very pleasant. They promptly got on the phone and activated the underground Vietnamese communication network. Later, I would come to understand that every immigrant group in every city in the world has a tangled web of connections that allows its members to locate one of their own within minutes. Nobody plans it – it just happens that way. But at the time, I thought it was an incredible coincidence that these people were able to get my uncles' phone number so quickly. As it turned out, they lived only fifteen minutes away. Soon they were knocking on the door, and Mother and I were reunited with Half-Uncle Trieu and Half-Uncle Nghia.

It was Half-Uncle Trieu who had used to take me for walks on the boardwalk by the Mekong and buy me smoothies while he wooed his girlfriend. All that seemed like a million years ago now, and in fact we had not seen my uncles since those days. I knew Half-Uncle Nghia even less well, but that was no matter. They were doing Mother a favour by agreeing to sponsor our entry to the US, and it was like a real family reunion. The brothers had been in America for over a year now, and they had already settled in with all the enthusiasm of young men who have good health, strong backs and their whole lives ahead of them.

Trieu and Nghia took us back to their two-bedroom apartment in Fullerton. The apartment was on the second floor facing the garden. My uncles showed us to our room, which was very simply furnished with a double bed. In the living room, there was a three-seater sofa, a low wooden coffee table and a small television. In the kitchen, there was little more than a dining table with four chairs. There were thick cream curtains on the windows to keep the sun and heat out.

Mother and I settled in slowly. We thought we were familiar with cities, but Saigon was nothing like Los Angeles. We had never seen so many automobiles in one place before. It seemed like there were millions of them. In Vietnam, only the very wealthy could afford a car. Here, even the poorest families had their own vehicle. The roads were well paved and broad in comparison with the national highways in Vietnam, which were still made of dirt, and on which the traffic – foot, bicycle, mobilette and bus – moved no faster than thirty or forty miles per hour. One of my first observations about America was that nobody walked – everybody drove. Petrol was so cheap.

Over the next few days, my uncles took us to the welfare office to register for health care. As a condition of our immigration status, which was that of permanent legal residency, Mother was required to attend English as a Second Language (ESL) courses and a job-training programme, while I was to go to school. We lost no time in getting signed up for all these things – we would sooner have died than not abide by the rules. My uncles, who had assembly-line jobs at an electronics manufacturing plant, bought Mother a scooter of her own. Within days, she had mastered the local streets and was able to transport herself to and from her classes without getting lost. I was proud and a little in awe of her ability to adapt. I thought of my mother and uncles as old, of course, but in fact Trieu and Nghia were only in their mid to late twenties, and while my mother was never exactly sure how old she was, at this time she could have been no more than thirty-five. They were all still young enough to adjust easily to a new life, especially one that offered so much promise. I wondered how long it would be before Mother had snagged her first American boyfriend.

Facing the apartment, there was another identical complex

where my uncles' friend was living alone in a one-bedroom apartment. He attended college in the daytime and worked part-time at night to pay his rent and other expenses. He came to visit us sometimes, and he and Mother would talk about their lives in Vietnam. Sometimes he stayed over for dinner. He really liked her cooking, because it had been a long time since he had eaten an authentic Vietnamese meal. There were only a few Vietnamese restaurants and stores in Orange County at the time.

I remember we had an American neighbour who lived right next door to us. He was a friendly man in his mid-thirties with short blond hair and big blue eyes. Sometimes he would smile and say hello when we bumped into each other outside on the balcony. Obviously he was not familiar with our culture, because he would knock on our door when my uncles spanked me for my bad behaviour. He could hear me crying from his apartment, and when he came to the door I could tell by the look on his face that he was shocked at the thought of an adult spanking a child, especially a girl.

I remember the first time I went into the supermarket with my uncles. The blast of cold air from the air conditioning hit me as the door opened, and I shivered, unused to the sensation. The floor was so clean that I could see my reflection in it, and the products were neatly organised on shelves. It could not have been more different to the bustle and colourful chaos of the markets back in Vietnam. The fruit and vegetables looked so fresh and shiny that I wanted to take a bite of them all. The meat was kept cold and free of any flies or insects, and the beef in particular looked so red that I could have eaten it raw. I noticed that there didn't seem to be any fresh fish or live fish like the ones I was used to seeing in the markets in Vietnam. I guessed that Americans were not fond of fish and its bones; they appeared to prefer them cleaned and kept frozen. There was also plenty of fresh milk, cheese, butter, yogurt and other dairy products that I had never seen before. I wandered around the vast aisles staring at everything with my mouth agape.

* * *

In September 1979, about two months after we arrived in the US, it was time for me to start school. One of my uncles took me there on the first day, but after that I was on my own, because they both had to work and Mother had English and training classes. The school was not far from where we lived, so I did not mind this too much.

After I arrived, I was taken to meet the school counsellors, who decided that I should enter the fourth grade. One of the office clerks then took me to my class and introduced me to the teacher. As I stood looking at the other children, I felt like an alien. I was twelve years old by this time – a bit too old to be hanging around with a bunch of nine and ten year olds. But physically I was the same size as they were, so none of my classmates were initially aware that I was in fact two or three years older than most of them, and I think that this helped me to blend in a little. Academically, however, I was far behind, and once I learned English I would have to catch up.

In Vietnam, our classrooms had been equipped with tables, chairs, pencils and paper. That was it. In America, there were technological marvels that I had never even heard of before, such as VCRs and overhead projectors. I was astounded at how the other students seemed to take these devices for granted. If someone in my village in Vietnam had owned a VCR, people would have come from miles around just to look at it – even though there would have been no electricity to run it.

There were also televisions, film projectors, cameras and – most of all – books. I had never been to a library before, and my new school had a nice one. It was with mixed pleasure and astonishment that I learned any student could check out any book he or she wanted, take it home, read it and then exchange it for another one – for free. It was a never-ending cycle of learning. The only limit was the student's own desire to learn.

Of course, this did me little good at the time, because I could not understand a word of English. Etymologically, English and Vietnamese have absolutely nothing in common, and I was not then, and am still not today, a gifted linguist. For months, therefore, I could understand only a few words. I was automatically enrolled in an ESL class, which was taught by an older American woman, her name was Mrs Taylor, I think. She was very friendly and helpful, and she had a lot of patience, which helped us tremendously as we struggled to acquire her native language.

But, as I have already said, I found English very difficult to learn, and I remember some months after I enrolled in school, a new Vietnamese boy came to our ESL class. He did not understand a single word of English, so Mrs Taylor asked me if I would translate as she tried to explain what she wanted him to do. Put on the spot like this, my mind went blank. I was confused and did not understand everything the teacher had said, but to save myself from the embarrassment of having to admit this, I just muttered something to the new boy. I can't even remember what I said, but he did not care anyway – he was like me, lost in this new world of strange people, language and culture. It was emotionally and physically exhausting, and often intimidating, but somehow we managed to keep going and adapted to our new environment, little by little, day after day.

I stayed at school for lunch at the cafeteria. It was free for me because we were on government aid. Lunches consisted of spaghetti, hamburgers, hot dogs, pizza, burritos and tacos, which were rotated on a daily basis. To drink, we had chocolate milk, which I guess was intended to help us grow. There was also salad and fresh fruit such as apples, oranges, grapes, bananas, peaches and strawberries, which I loved. I had never seen grapes, strawberries or peaches before, and back home in Vietnam, apples were considered to be a very special treat, as they had to be imported from Western countries. Occasionally, when Mother would make one of her trips back to Huu Dinh, she would bring me an apple. When this happened, I would hold it and smell it for hours, as it was such a luxury.

Despite my struggles with English, I still had my flair for self-teaching, and it was this that enabled me to achieve my first academic success. One day, the whole class was assigned to write a report on something I happened to know a lot about: water. Initially, I had no idea what I needed to do to complete the assignment, but luckily, my determination to learn kicked in. There was, of course, plenty I could have said about this topic. I could have written pages about the ancient legend of the battle between Thuy Tinh and Son Tinh, for example. I could have explained how I had fallen into the Mekong as a child and how I first felt the water god's hands trying to pull me under, as if he wanted me to replace his lost love, the Princess My Nuong. I could have gone on to describe our boat journey to Malaysia and talked about how I had watched as that poor pregnant woman's body was tossed over the side and sank into the water god's realm – a sacrifice to him and a symbol of all that we had lost.

But my English wasn't good enough to say any of this, and I felt sure that nobody would be interested anyway. I had already sensed that America was not a land of legends and magic but a place where people wanted everything done right away and where nobody liked to waste time on old stories. I thought to myself that people would just laugh at me – and, besides, I wanted to forget the tragedies of my life. Therefore, instead of explaining my Vietnamese understanding of water to my American teacher, I spent hours trying to decipher – with the help of a thick Vietnamese–English dictionary – the strange glyphs in an encyclopaedia so that I could understand the American version of water for myself. It was dry and boring: all about hydrogen and oxygen, watersheds, irrigation, evaporation and rainfall. America did not have any interesting water stories. There was no spiritual connection to this most vital of all the earth's gifts, no respect for this most frightening of all elements. There were just facts and statistics, and that was what passed for truth.

Somehow, however, I was able to compile this information into a 500-word essay. I did the work all on my own, and my teacher thought it was good enough to enter into a city-wide essay contest. Then, to my surprise and delight – and not without a certain sense of irony – I won first prize for my grade level.

Mother and my uncles shared my happiness. It was a sign, they said, of all the great things I would achieve in our new country. But then came scary news: I would have to read my paper aloud, on television, for a programme that would be broadcast into all the classrooms in the county. I didn't think there was any way I could do it – speaking English was like talking with a mouthful of rocks. I could barely pronounce the few words I knew. But Mrs Taylor and I drilled and drilled, and when the big day came and I was standing in front of a television camera for the first time in my life, I made it through in one take. My only criticism of my performance, as I watched it later, did not concern my speaking skills but the fact that I kept tossing my head to get the hair out of my eyes. I felt it made me look childish.

It was my first triumph, but it was also to be my last for a long, long time. After the excitement of living in America began to wear off, I found myself sinking back into the unhappiness that had haunted me my whole life. I had new reasons to hate myself now: I was a boat person, an undesirable; a tiny, undernourished, dark-skinned Asian girl in a land of huge, well-fed white people. I felt intimidated by this difference and at times felt that people were looking down on me.

I also found it hard to adapt to the new culture into which I had been thrust. Everything in America seemed to move so fast, as though everyone were on a relentless treadmill. Basically, people woke up, washed, got into their cars, drove to work, did their jobs, then came home, ate and went to bed to get some sleep before waking up the next day and going through the same routine. Nobody seemed to have time to talk to each other or take an interest in each other as they had done back at home. Vietnam may be a poor country but the Vietnamese people are genuine and caring, with kind hearts. Things seemed very different in my new home, and I often felt homesick for my simple village life in Vietnam.

I could have sought help from my teachers, but the language

barrier prevented me from doing so. I also assumed that they wouldn't understand what I was feeling, because they were all white. I also figured that, to some extent, they must be having problems themselves, adjusting to the wave of boat people who had ended up in their country after their unexpected loss of a devastating war.

There were other Vietnamese children in school, and some of them had had similar experiences of fleeing the Communist regime. But we didn't communicate much. I think we were all experiencing similar feelings of displacement and bewilderment as we struggled to adjust to our new lives, and it was difficult for any of us to talk about what we had been through. It also soon became clear that some of the American students resented our presence and the government assistance we were getting, such as welfare for low-income families and free medical care. Others were simply racist. I reacted to all this in the same way I had always reacted when faced with difficult social situations: I withdrew. I began to gain a reputation for being standoffish and rebuffed every attempt at friendship. Soon, the other students stopped trying, and I was left to wallow in my loneliness. I didn't understand my behaviour then, and I'm still not sure that I understand it completely today. But I think that deep inside I was worried about getting hurt. I was scared that if I opened up to others about the way I was feeling, they might let me down. I was scared of not being liked, of being abandoned – of so many things. These fears prevented me from making new friends, and I found it difficult to communicate with other people.

Typically, as it seemed to me at the time, my mother either didn't notice what was going on with me or else she wanted to pretend that everything was all right. I think now that it was more likely the latter. Considering the miraculous fact that we were still alive, I can't blame her in the slightest for wanting to make the most of her new situation, to focus on the good things that were happening to us and not to waste time worrying about things that might go wrong, or about her difficult, ungrateful daughter. She didn't seem to have the time or patience to draw me out, which was what I needed most. I was a self-teacher but not a self-healer. I never felt close to my mother, and I never felt that I could talk to her about my problems. Nor did my uncles offer any comfort, as I think they saw me as a very difficult, unappreciative child.

I do not deny that much of my misery was self-inflicted. After all, thinking about it now, my mother's life had been even harder than mine in many ways, and yet she had maintained a positive attitude through it all. I thought that my struggle to settle into my new environment was just another sign that there was something wrong with me. Caught in this vicious emotional cycle, I became more and more unhappy.

Mother, meanwhile, had got herself a job as a seamstress in a clothes factory. She was paid $3.50 per hour – a fortune in comparison to what she had made sewing ao dai back home. Of course, the cost of living in America was much higher, too. As strange as it sounds, there are some economic benefits to living in a developing country, one of them being that you can live on practically no money. Here in America, Mother had no choice – she had to make lots of money if we were ever going to get out on our own. For now, though, we continued to share one bedroom in the little apartment while my uncles slept in the other.

My uncles had adapted with great enthusiasm to the car culture of America in general, and of California in particular. With the money they were making at the electronics plant, they bought themselves something that only a millionaire in Vietnam could have dreamed of possessing: a white two-seater GM convertible. It was a beautiful machine that even I fell in love with. Whenever they had days off, they used to just hop in and go, and if I didn't have to go to school I went with them. The car could only hold two adults, but I was so small that I fitted perfectly behind the seats, as if I were a piece of luggage. It was unsafe, but coming from a country that had no legal safety standards, that didn't bother us at all.

We didn't just go for spins around the block. We took long camping trips – the further away the better. We drove all the way up the coast to Redwood National State Park, spending endless blissful hours on Highway 1, a two-lane road that hugs the stunning Californian coastline for hundreds of miles. We owned no camping equipment, naturally, so we simply slept on the ground. I was small enough that I could actually crawl under the car to protect myself from the dew. We went to Yosemite National Park, Las Vegas and the Hoover Dam – all journeys of hundreds of miles. But petrol cost very little, my uncles were young men and all three of us were in awe of the vastness that is the American West.

No one who has seen the massive spaces of America can remain unmoved by the experience. To us, who had started out as simple, uneducated Third-Worlders, it was as if we had passed into another dimension altogether. Once, however, when my uncles invited me along on a trip to the Grand Canyon, my so-called 'second sight' began to tingle. I hadn't felt it so strongly since the last time I sat in my step-grandfather's cinema in Ben Tre. I refused to go with them, without providing any explanation. A few days later, my uncles called to say that I had been right not to come: they had lost control of the car, rolled it and totalled it. If I had been sitting in the back, where I wouldn't even have had a proper seat belt, I would have been killed.

Other teenagers might have been badly shaken by a near miss like this, but after surviving missile attacks and a shipwreck, I barely gave it a second thought.

Little by little, Mother and I got used to California. We found the weather greatly to our liking, of course – more temperate than that of Vietnam, but still nice and warm, with lots of sunshine. Strange mysteries and customs began to reveal themselves to us. You had to obey traffic signs. Policemen were not to be bribed. Garbage was collected on a regular basis by men in large trucks. You could drive up to a window and order food. If you didn't like something about the government, you were allowed to discuss it openly, without fear of reprisal. And so on.

Life proceeded day by day, each one filled with strange discoveries and new challenges. We were thrilled every time we discovered or heard of new Vietnamese restaurants or stores opening somewhere in Orange County, and Mother would take me there to see what they were selling. It was a good way for Mother to meet other Vietnamese in town and helped us feel some kind of connection to home.

Sometimes, we went to the malls nearby to shop for new clothes. I used to like Wet Seal, a fashionable shop for teenage girls, and I loved eating warm and moist Mother's Cookies and sipping strawberry icee. But throughout this time I failed to make any new friends and convinced myself that I was happier on my own. I didn't feel lonely, but when I was at the mall, watching other teenagers talking, eating and shopping with their friends, I felt a bit left out. It was only at those times that I wished I could have a real friend to spend time with – someone who would understand and accept me for who I was.

Before I knew it, it was time for me to enter junior high school. By this point, Mother had found herself a new boyfriend, who she met at one of her ESL classes, and things between them got serious enough that she and I left my uncles and moved in with him. This was the start of a long pattern of relocation based on my mother's affairs of the heart. I was never consulted; I was still not old enough to have a say in the matter.

This boyfriend, Minh, had two children, a girl and a boy, who were being fostered by an American Christian family somewhere. He had been married, but I don't know if he was now divorced or whether his wife had died back in Vietnam. I did not know how long he had been living in America, and, to be honest, we hardly talked to each other, as I didn't imagine that we would be staying with him for long.

Minh had a two-bedroom apartment in Anaheim. At first I

hoped this meant that I would finally have my own room, but, in fact, the second bedroom was already occupied by his nephew, who was aged about eighteen. I know now that in American families it's more likely that in such a situation the girl would be given the bedroom. But Vietnamese families have different priorities: in general, boys are more important than girls. So, I slept on the couch in the living room. I felt very resentful about this, as not only was I forced to move against my will but my living conditions were also downgraded. I had always rated at least a bed, even in the refugee camp. Now, I felt as if I was being treated like a piece of excess baggage. I could have spoken out and told Mother how I felt, but I didn't think there was any point. I was sure that she would never jeopardise her new relationship just to keep me happy.

I now attended seventh-grade classes at Brookhurst Junior High School, which was a good thirty-minute walk from our new home. I hated this journey, as I had to cross a bridge built over the freeway. But I liked the school, which was quiet, clean and spacious.

I finally made a friend, too – Isidora, a Mexican girl who was just as homesick as I was. Isidora was sweet, kind and gentle, and often invited me to her home, where she would cook Mexican food for us. I loved her cooking. Being so salty and spicy, it often reminded me of Asian food, yet it had a flavour all of its own. I loved tacos, quesadillas, burritos and enchiladas, all stuffed with beef, chicken or pork, plus Isidora's colourful Spanish rice and nacho chips with salsa and guacamole. I thought back to the smell of stir-fried duck with rice that the old woman in Ben Tre had cooked across the alleyway from Half-Uncle Hong's house. To me, that old woman had symbolised cleanliness and order amidst the chaos of my life, and I had longed to join her. Finally, sitting in Isidora's kitchen, listening to her chattering away to her mother in Spanish, I felt as if I had managed to cross over into a Mexican-American version of that clean, delicious world.

Besides our homesickness and our love of food, Isidora and I had something else in common – dark skin. One day, as we were walking home from school along Brookhurst Street, we decided to stop and rest on the kerb in front of a house in a nice residential area. But within a minute, the homeowner came out and chased us away. There was no doubt in our minds as to why this had happened. We were the wrong colour and therefore were likely up to no good. Our assumption might have been wrong, but that was what we believed at the time. Burning with shame, we ran. I never went back through that neighbourhood for fear of being arrested, or worse.

I knew that in America everybody was supposed to be treated the same and that all people were held to be created equal. But incidents like this reminded me of the prejudice and favouritism that had been exercised by the Communists at my old school in Huu Dinh. I was incredibly sensitive to such issues and felt disappointed that nowhere was free from discrimination – not even the great nation of America.

Meanwhile, at school, I had developed a fondness for my mathematics teacher, Miss Yoko, a Japanese-American woman. My ESL teacher had been a great help, but Miss Yoko was really the first person in my life to help me begin to develop my intellectual abilities. She had an easy, clear way of explaining things that even I could understand, and through her, I discovered something amazing about myself: I had a photographic memory. I could look at a page, take a picture of it and remember it for ever, storing it in my brain for as long as I needed it. As she taught me to master this ability, my test scores began to improve immediately, and, as a result, my self-esteem slowly began to improve.

It was also at this time that my social circle finally began to expand. Minh's nephew was a member of a Vietnamese Scouting group, and he managed to convince me to attend a meeting with him. I was reluctant at first, but finally I agreed to go, and I had a great time. I started attending regularly, and we met once a week in a community park, where we sang songs, learned Morse code, had scavenger hunts and made plans for future excursions. We communicated in our native language and sang Vietnamese songs. I was shy about singing out loud, because I was not a very good singer. The group teased me that my singing voice could wake up the mosquitoes. Scouting was a good way to preserve something of the life that we had left behind in Vietnam, and it also gave me a great opportunity to learn a lot more about my own culture.

To my astonishment, there were two girls in the group whom I recognised from the camp in Malaysia. I was further shocked to learn that they had actually been on the same boat as Mother and I, and had lost their parents in the shipwreck.

One might have thought that I would become close friends with these girls, but in fact we didn't have much to do with each other. Orphans in a strange land, they were still grieving the loss of their parents and trying hard to adjust to life with their new American foster parents. It was very painful for them to discuss anything to do with the journey by sea, the shipwreck or the camp. I understand this now, but at the time I felt hurt because they didn't make any effort to be friends with me. Perhaps they did not like my attitude, or they were just too busy with their own friends. Whatever the reason, it reinforced my feeling that there was something wrong with me, and I was hurt by what I took to be their rejection.

In truth, I did not make any close friends in my Scouting troop; I was just one of the crowd. I was still very shy and withdrawn, and I found it difficult to start conversations with people I didn't know. As a result, the reputation that I had gained at school for being standoffish carried over to the Scout troop.

I also felt resentful of the older girls, who were all tall, slim and pretty. Even though I had finally managed to start gaining weight, I had yet to start growing upwards – so now, instead of being short and skinny, I was short and chubby – thanks to the many fast-food chains in California such as McDonald's, Kentucky Fried Chicken, Taco Bell, In and Out, Carl's Junior, Pizza Hut – the list goes on.

All the boys liked the tall, thin girls, while I was completely ignored. I had never been beautiful by Vietnamese standards, but there was a tiny part of me that had hoped things would somehow be different in America. Now, though, I was finding out that this was not to be. No matter where in the world I went, I realised, I would still be me – short, fat, ugly and unpopular.

I desperately needed to make a connection with somebody. Like everyone else on the planet, I needed to feel loved. And now that I was an adolescent, it wouldn't be long until I started looking in another direction for that affection: boys.

8

Life in America

At the end of 1982, my mother, who had been diligent about following her training courses, found a job that just a few years earlier she never could have imagined herself doing: working as an electrician in a shipyard in Long Beach. The work was demanding and the hours long, but the pay was good. She began bringing home even more money. In a short time, she had succeeded in adapting to American culture to a degree that anyone who knew her back home in Vietnam would have found unbelievable. That's my mother – she doesn't just survive. She shines.

Yet my mother's role within our so-called 'family' was still very much a traditional, old-fashioned one. And our living situation continued to get worse, not better. Early in 1983, two of Minh's nieces came to live with us from Vietnam, via a refugee camp. The nephew who had introduced me to Scouting moved out, but there was another, younger, nephew waiting to take his place. He got the second bedroom all to himself, while I and these two new, strange girls – who, as refugees themselves, were no doubt facing their own emotional challenges – slept in the living room. They adapted very quickly to their new life in America and didn't appear to have the same problems as I had had in settling in.

In this expanding household, my mother was expected to do all the cooking and cleaning – for everyone. And although my mother herself never questioned this, I was enraged by it. I helped her clean the house, because I could not stand dirt – I was a cleaning freak. But no one else lifted a finger to help her, except when

Minh would do the cooking while my mother was at work.

Maybe I was already more American than I realised, as one day, fed up with the shabby treatment Mother was receiving, I threw a tantrum, kicking the coffee table over and screaming at everyone that my mother was not to be thought of as a maid. Of course, everyone was appalled at my behaviour – including Mother. Vietnamese females are not supposed to act like that; they're supposed to be meek and docile, fulfilling their domestic functions and obeying orders without question. Much the same expectations exist for children in general, who are thought of as more like pets than people. Although I had a problem with this attitude even before we left Vietnam, now I was in a country where women were encouraging each other to throw off the shackles of domesticity and assert themselves in whatever way they chose. I don't remember how conscious I was of the feminist movement, but certainly I was already conducting my own private gender rebellion even back in Huu Dinh – and now, in the most progressive state in the wealthiest country in the world, I had plenty of outside influences, both subliminal and conscious, to egg me on.

California had been an exciting place ever since gold was first discovered there – at around the same time as Marx and Engels wrote their *Communist Manifesto* and the French began to colonise Vietnam. Now, more than 130 years later, it was seen as the source of everything new and trendy. California's important position in the American psyche had begun long ago, with the advent of the film industry, but it had been cemented by the creation of MTV, which, for the first time, gave young people an instant visual connection to their pop idols and literally changed the way they saw the world – and themselves. The vast majority of videos were shot and produced in southern California, and numerous famous musical acts got their start there and spread outward. Culturally, SoCal was the epicentre of an earthquake.

I don't mean to say that I was aware of all this at the time. But now, looking back, I can see that I was living in a culture that was enthralled with its own youthfulness and virility. Everyone else in the developed world was paying attention to what was going on in California, and the excitement was being generated by male and female influences alike. There may still have been inequalities in how the genders were treated behind the scenes, but all we saw on TV was women dressing outrageously and doing whatever they wanted. Madonna, Cyndi Lauper, The Bangles, The Go-Gos, Grace Jones, Kate Bush . . . even if one wasn't paying any attention at all, there was still a strong subconscious effect from these liberated women, who were there every time you turned on the television.

I was not punished for this outburst; instead, my mother simply ignored it. I was now fifteen years old, which meant that on top of being my natural, disagreeable self, I was hormonal. Despite all we had been through together, my mother and I were not what you would have called close, and I didn't feel that I could turn to her about things that were going on. When I began to menstruate at the age of fourteen, for example, I wasn't particularly comfortable having to tell her about it. I knew what was happening to me through conversations that I had overheard between women back in Vietnam and also through programmes I had seen on the television, and, once a month, flushed with shame, I went to the store on my own and bought myself some tampons, always making sure to choose a female cashier. But hitting puberty American-style wasn't all bad. I could only imagine what the women in rural Vietnam had to use during their periods, as they certainly wouldn't have had access to the Western sanitary products now available to me.

I also began to feel some sexual curiosity, but again there was no one to whom I could talk about it. My mother had never mentioned a thing about sex to me. However, Minh had a cable subscription that included an adult channel, so once more I displayed my knack for self-teaching: I learned about the birds and the bees in stolen moments of watching complete strangers do it on screen. Later, in the bathtub, I experimented with touching myself the way the people in those movies touched each other. I discovered that my body had secrets to teach me, and I set about learning them, one by one.

Soon, Mother and I received news that we were going to be uprooted again. Yet more relatives of Minh's were due to arrive from Vietnam, and Minh's own children, who had been living with a white family out of state in order to become 'Americanised', were soon going to be moving back with him, too. Even by Vietnamese standards, the overcrowding would have been too much, and as Mother and I were not relations, and as there was no sign that Minh intended to marry my mother, we had to go.

Although I had been unhappy living with Minh, I had a very dramatic reaction to this news and threw a huge temper tantrum. This time, however, I didn't do it in public, where I could embarrass my mother and myself. Instead, when I was alone, I smashed my head into the wall several times. It was very painful, and I felt dizzy and sick. So I sat down, resting my forehead on my knees, trying to get control of myself. I had been temped to do this before, but this day I was pushed to my limits.

I knew right away that I had gone too far in my self-abuse. Something in my head didn't feel right. It was several minutes before the feeling passed and I could stand up again, but I was still unsteady on my feet.

I went to bed early that night. In the morning, when I got up, I vomited into the bathroom sink, and I had a splitting headache all that day. Gradually it faded, but it was to come back repeatedly, and with a vengeance. Something in my brain had been altered and not in a good way. Now it seems clear that I must have had concussion and could even have suffered brain damage, but there was no question of me telling anyone what I had done, as I was too scared about what the reaction would have been.

I would continue to suffer repercussions from this incident both in the immediate aftermath and for years to come. Prior to this episode, I had had a photographic memory. I was also good with numbers and analytical thinking. In the weeks and months that followed my self-inflicted head injury, my ability to take a mental snapshot of a page in an instant disappeared, never to return. I also lost a great deal of my ability to reason mathematically. My short-term memory was affected and sometimes, in conversation with my peers, I would forget that we had just discussed a particular subject and bring it up all over again. This was obviously irritating to those around me, and I got a reputation for being a rather stupid and boring person.

Why did I smash my head into the wall? On the surface, the answer seems simple – I didn't want to move again. I just wanted to stay in one place for a while. We had faced down death, disease and despair to make it to America and create a new home for ourselves. Yet even though we had achieved the impossible and actually survived the journey, it seemed our place on this earth was still every bit as tenuous as it had been back in Ben Tre. Mother and I were of no more value than two pieces of battered furniture. When the house became too crowded, we were simply tossed out. This realisation was more than I could take. I was in such pain emotionally that I mirrored it physically; I was trying to show the world how worthless I really felt. When no one then noticed what had happened to me, it only reinforced these feelings. Even Miss Yoko, my favourite teacher, didn't try to find out what had happened when my results as school suddenly suffered, but I guess she might have thought that I was just being lazy and falling behind with my homework.

With nowhere else to go, we decided to move back in with Half-Uncle Trieu and Half-Uncle Nghia. By now, the brothers had left Fullerton and moved to a larger place in Anaheim, which was a good thing, as we weren't the only new guests who were coming to stay. Two of my half-aunts and a cousin were coming from Hong Kong, where they had been living in a refugee camp – by all accounts a much nicer one than the one in which we had stayed in Malaysia. They were part of Step-Grandfather Thanh's family. Being wealthy, they had enjoyed a relatively smooth exit from Vietnam – no doubt due to the payment of bribes – and a shipwreck-free journey across the sea in a boat that was designed to hold plenty of people. I dreaded their arrival, since Thanh's family had always tended to look down on Mother and me. They were richer and more educated, and it seemed to me that they thought Mother and I were just country peasants. But, as usual, there was nothing we could do about it, except to take what life handed us and make the best of things.

Now fifteen years old, and having been allowed to skip the eighth grade by the principal at Brookhurst, I entered the ninth grade at Anaheim High School. I lost touch with my friend Isidora at this stage, as she went to a different school, and I missed spending time at her home with her warm and welcoming family. I was sad to leave her behind, but, thankfully, I was able to make new friends at this school.

There were two tall, thin Vietnamese sisters in some of my classes, and we would sit at the same table at lunch in the cafeteria and chat during our short breaks in between classes. At the weekends, we would play tennis and go to parties together, and they invited me to eat at their home when their mother was cooking. We had lots of fun together, but their nickname for me was *be bu*, which means 'short and fat'. They didn't say this to be cruel and probably thought it wouldn't bother me because it's normal for Vietnamese people to tease in this way. But I was already so conscious of the way I looked that I found it very hurtful. I don't know what was worse – their teasing, or the taunts I was subjected to at home by my aunts, one of whom said – to my face – that I would no doubt grow up to be ugly and repulsive. Then she had the nerve to laugh. She herself was tall and pretty, of course, just like everyone in the world, it seemed – except me.

I also made another Vietnamese friend in my Scout troop, Hoi An. Her mother had named her after the well-known city in Central Vietnam where she was born. Hoi An loved to play tennis, and she talked me into playing with her after school. We went regularly to the tennis courts of California State University, Fullerton, with her older sister, but I was never very good.

A while later, I met Thu, a bright girl in one of my classes. Thu had a sister who was a grade higher and one of the best singers in the school's music group. Thu's sister received scholarships to continue her education and career in singing, and her family formed a Vietnamese musical band, which organised monthly music and dancing events in the Vietnamese community. Mother and I went to see her family's band play a few times on special occasions such as Tet and major holidays in America such as Christmas. I was getting better at making friends among my own community, but I still found it too difficult to break out of this circle and make any friends from the wider school network.

When I was fifteen, I met my first boyfriend, E, at a weekend party I went to with the girls. E was eighteen and good-looking. More importantly, he was a gentle guy and genuinely nice to me. E had a reputation as a good DJ, which meant he was popular at parties. At first, I asked him if he would come to visit me as a friend at my school during lunch-time sometimes. After that, he and I went out to parties where he was invited to play as DJ on weekends. We also went to see movies together, and ate popcorn and drank Coke – things that all American teenagers do. We had lots of fun together. I also discovered that E was immensely knowledgeable about cars. He could talk about all makes of cars and their features for hours. On long weekends, we would drive up to Lake Elsinore and sometimes Lake Perris with his friends for the day, and we would have a picnic and play outdoor games.

After we had been dating for a few months, I invited E home and introduced him to my mother. She seemed happy that I had made some new friends, and she placed no restrictions on my movements and activities with him.

One of my clearest memories of my adolescence is of wearing a light pink party dress and slow-dancing with E while the stereo played 'Put Your Head On My Shoulder'. The occasion was my sixteenth birthday, on 5 August 1983, and I held a huge birthday party at a clubhouse in the condominium where we lived. I invited most of the boys and girls in my Scout troop, my uncles and aunts, my cousins, my friends at school, E and his friends. It was a magical day for both of us.

Out in the dark next to the pool, we kissed and touched each other out of sight of the other guests, but that was as far as things went. I was still a virgin, and so was E, although I didn't know it at the time – I simply assumed that because he was older, he was also more experienced. But E really was an unusual person. He never pressured me into anything, and he embodied a great many of the most admirable characteristics of Vietnamese culture.

E was renting a bedroom in a townhouse near Little Saigon, as he had come to the US on his own without his family. When I visited him there, we would drive to Huntington and Newport Beach with one of his roommates, The. The was a weightlifting fanatic, and he had huge muscles. I had a secret crush on him, although my heart belonged to E. Sometimes we went fishing at night on the pier or boardwalk, although I never seemed to catch any fish. Despite my fear of water, I still loved to walk along the beach at night, thinking about what I had been through far away on the other side of the ocean. Although I would often cry, remembering my sister and the shipwreck, this released some of the tension I constantly felt inside.

Little by little, because of this healthy and positive first relationship, I began to enjoy myself.

A few months later, we received word that my grandmother and the rest of my cousin's family would be coming from Hong Kong. They were to move in with my uncles. Grandmother, Mother's mother, had married Thanh after her husband was executed for spying; now she was leaving Vietnam because all her children were going. Cultural mores dictated that they should not leave her behind, since in our society we care for our parents in the home until the day they die. Thanh himself was staying in Vietnam with one of his other wives – not that what he did mattered to us one way or the other. But Mother and I were once again on the bottom of the totem pole, and so we had to move out. I was beginning to feel as if my days as a refugee had never really ended. Only the location had changed.

We found a bedroom to rent in an apartment belonging to a young couple in Westminster. They had a small baby, and they seemed like nice people. But things quickly turned sour when it became clear that they wanted to pinch every penny until it screamed, to the point where we were literally not allowed to turn on the lights. Mother and I didn't think we were princesses, but we did think that we had the right to see where we were going, so after a few months with them, we moved out again.

By now, Mother had saved up enough money to make a down payment on a two-bedroom condo in Tustin, and I finished up the tenth grade at Ocean View High School. Something had happened by this point to end things between Minh and Mother. I never understood why they broke up, but it wasn't long before Mother found a new boyfriend and I heard that he was to move in with us in our new home. His name was Dung, meaning courage. He spelled his name the same way as I did, but it was pronounced differently, which in Vietnamese makes it a different name altogether. I had only met this man a few times at the house of one of my mother's friends, and usually I would have been upset about the situation, but at that point I didn't care, as I was too excited about the fact that finally, after four years in America, I was about to have a room of my own.

I was in heaven. I had teddy bears everywhere in my room and decorated the walls with posters of Rick Springfield, Olivia Newton-John and photos of beautiful women cut out from fashion magazines. I knew I would never look like them, but it comforted me to see them and to know that somewhere in the world, something was perfect. Finally, I began to feel like a real American teenager.

It was also at this time that I did something else that other American teenagers were doing: I lost my virginity. I'm not saying it was unheard of to have sex before marriage in Vietnam, but it would never have been discussed. In America, I was amazed at how brash and frank girls were in talking about their sexuality. I never completely adjusted to this, because I was brought up to believe it was bad manners. But I went ahead and did it anyway.

My first, however, was not E. I found him sweet and gentle, but he didn't excite me the way I wanted to be excited, at least not sexually. We rarely saw each other now and had pretty much broken up, so, instead, I made love for the first time with a young man, M. I met M at a friend's birthday party. He was a tall, thin boy, equally polite as E but with a more developed sense of how to treat a girl. He was also more compassionate and thoughtful than E. He often brought me presents, which bowled me over, but our relationship was far from perfect and was even a little strange.

For example, on one occasion he took me to his house to meet his mother and sister, but, puzzlingly, he never actually introduced me to them. They treated me quite coldly, which I interpreted as meaning that they thought M could do better – although I never knew why. Maybe they wanted M to date a white girl. His sister was dating a young man in the US Army, which was considered very prestigious. Or maybe it was because word of my bad, un-Vietnamese-like behaviour had already reached them through the underground Vietnamese communication network. As if to confirm their suspicions, my relationship with M was very fiery. I screamed at him and shouted, and I was jealous and suspicious. All in all, I never treated him with respect. I did not know why I was behaving this way and thought it must be because I was really in love this time. I was still emotionally very immature and thought only of my own feelings. I knew that M was disappointed in me when I behaved this way, but I was unable to stop myself.

About two months after our first date, our first love-making session took place late one night, completely by surprise. M stood outside my bedroom window and threw pebbles at the glass until I let him in. He then grabbed me, kissed me, carried me up the stairs to my bedroom and made love to me. I can't remember, but I guess my mother and her boyfriend must have been either out or asleep. I wasn't completely sure how I felt about the experience, or what I thought about M, but we continued to see each other and sleep together for several months.

Now seventeen, I enrolled in yet another school – Tustin High School – for the eleventh grade. Mother's boyfriend, Dung, was living with us by now, and he and Mother were trying to figure out how they could get ahead financially. The logical answer was for them to kick me out of my bedroom, move me into the living room and rent out my old room to an ancient Pakistani man they had run into somewhere who needed a place to stay.

I had been through rather a lot in my life thus far, and the fact that I was being booted out of the only place in which I'd felt safe since leaving Huu Dinh was more than I could take. I didn't just get mad. I lost it. I screamed horrible disrespectful things at my mother and Dung, and then Dung and I got into a fight. We wrestled on the couch. I don't think he tried to hit me, but I certainly tried to hit him, and he had to pin me down to prevent me. This was the worst blow-up to date in my relationship with my mother, and, if I might be so bold, it was possibly the most audacious thing any female member of my family had ever attempted in the last thousand years. In Vietnam, a child simply does not yell at her parents, or, in fact, at any adult, ever – period.

But we weren't in Vietnam any more and none of us – Mother, me, or Dung – really had the slightest idea what the rules were any more. My fight with Dung was so bad that the neighbours were pounding on the walls, and my mother was horrified. She seemed to think that the whole situation was my fault and kept ranting that I was a wilful, stupid, stubborn, ungrateful, disobedient little girl, and my ancestors would be ashamed of me. She had made her point and I was mad. So the next day, I did what any good American girl in a dramatic music video on MTV would have done.

I ran away.

9

Runaway

Although my argument with Mother's latest boyfriend was not our first, it was definitely our worst. And the thought of some strange old man sleeping amongst my fashion-model pictures and teddy bears was too much. I didn't feel the slightest guilt in disappearing the next day. After all, Dung wasn't my father, and it seemed obvious to me that my mother didn't care about me, so why should I care about either of them? I was old enough to take care of myself. If we were still living in Vietnam, I might even have been married already. Plus, I had been through more in my life than ten normal American girls put together. I had no doubt I could handle any kind of situation I might find myself in.

I was still seeing M at this point, but there was no way I could turn to him, as his family would never have agreed to let me stay with them. I was also still in touch with E, and we saw each other as friends now and again, but because he had a roommate, I chose not to go to him for sanctuary. One of the things I wanted was privacy, after all, so I turned to another friend, Xuan, a girl I had met at a party where E was DJing one night.

I thought Xuan was really cool because she lived in an apartment in Pomona with her boyfriend and a group of friends and acquaintances who ranged in age from fifteen to twenty-five. Also, she dyed her hair red and wore lots of crazy, Madonna-inspired make-up, as did many of the other people in the house. I knew little about Xuan's personal life, or how she had come to be living in the apartment, and I didn't know much about the other people in the house, either. But their independent lifestyle

127

greatly appealed to me. Vietnamese culture was strict, but here there were no boundaries at all – it was the complete opposite of what I was used to.

So, I left Mother and Dung without a word of farewell and moved into the apartment in Pomona with Xuan. I was too excited about moving out to care that I had no idea how I was going to survive or feed myself. I had a hundred dollars in my pocket, and I was sure that I would find some way to get by. I could get a part-time job at a fast-food outlet if I had to. It wasn't hard for high-school students to find minimum-wage part-time jobs.

For the two weeks my anarchical social experiment lasted, it was ideal. I stopped attending school and spent all day hanging out with Xuan and my new friends. Nearly all the kids in the house were Vietnamese, which meant that most of them were survivors of the war and now presumably struggling with the same issues of cultural integration that I was.

None of us would have phrased it that way, of course. We didn't think we had any problems in America – especially now we were free from the influence of our parents. We did whatever we wanted. But looking back now, I can see that we were just young kids desperately trying to figure out how we fitted into this world we'd been thrown into. We'd had to leave Vietnam to escape the war, and believed that in America we would be leaving the dream. But it wasn't that easy to adjust, and instead of integrating easily into American society, we clung together and formed our own community. The same thing happened when we ran away from home, even though it was the traditions, rules, constricting taboos and rigid dictates of our Vietnamese culture that we were trying to escape.

It's sad to think that this apartment in Pomona was really nothing but a microcosm of a shattered society, a temporary way station for a lot of lost souls who were going from nowhere to nowhere. Ten years after the war had ended, we were all still living like refugees. Nevertheless, this house provided me a temporary escape where I could take shelter for a few days – until my troubles were gone and forgotten.

There was no constant population in the apartment. New people came and went every day. We ate ramen noodles for every meal, and we went to parties every night. These parties were huge, and they were always fun, but I didn't allow myself to get out of control like some of the kids did. I wasn't into drinking or drugs – I didn't taste a drop of alcohol until I was twenty-one – and casual sex was not my thing, either.

While I was away from home, I did not see either M or E. But I did meet a boy who was half-Vietnamese and half-German, with whom I thought I had a connection. We slept together once, but I cried the whole time, without really knowing why. It wasn't because I was in physical pain. It must have been the feeling that I was teetering on the edge of some kind of abyss, and although I would rather have died than admit it to anyone, I was deeply scared of what was going to happen to me.

I must admit, looking back, that my life could have gone in a bad direction from there. That was what happened to a lot of kids in my situation. Running away is the first step on a slippery slope that often leads to drug and alcohol abuse, casual sex and violence, petty crime, trouble with the police, addiction, early pregnancy, or any of the other common factors that go into creating a life of poverty and abuse. I'm sure plenty of the kids I was hanging out with got into far worse trouble in the years ahead.

But before this could happen to me, something terrible occurred that woke me up and made me realise I was at serious risk. I hadn't known it at the time, perhaps because I was really oblivious to what was going on all around me, but a lot of the kids who were living in that apartment were gang members. They supported themselves through crime, and they often engaged in fights with rival gangs. One night, one of the boys was shot and killed, and as a result the police came in force and tore the entire place apart, looking for anything illegal. We all ended up at the police station, where we were fingerprinted, photographed and questioned. When they asked who I was, I just told them that I'd happened to be at the apartment looking for a friend. It never occurred to them that I was a runaway. I didn't know anything worth telling them, so they let me go.

This event was all I needed to convince me that life in that house was a dead end. But I still wasn't ready to go back to Mother, nor had I any desire to resume life on the living-room couch while some nasty old man got to sleep in my bed. So, I said goodbye to Xuan and moved with another girlfriend into a student apartment block at the University of California – Irvine (UCI).

This was possible because there were no resident assistants or other authority figures present, and one more Asian girl on a university campus would easily go unnoticed, especially if she carried a couple of books around and kept herself to herself. Life here was certainly quieter than it had been in the gang house. I was now surrounded by girls who were all studying to be engineers, doctors, lawyers and the like. But they had no use for me, an ignorant high-school dropout and runaway, and it showed in their standoffish behaviour. But I managed to get along by keeping myself out of their way when they were back from classes. Most of the day, they were on campus attending classes and studying in the university library. They were a quiet but intelligent crowd.

I stayed in the apartment for another two weeks. During this time, I got back in touch with E, and he came to see me. No longer was I the demure, virginal girl he remembered. Now, I was an experienced girl of the streets, or so I thought. I took him to bed with me in this strange apartment and showed him the things I had learned. But he was still a virgin, and I think he was rather traumatised by our encounter and by the changes he saw in me because soon after that we stopped seeing each other for good.

After two weeks, my mother found out where I was – no doubt using the trusty old underground Vietnamese communication network – and she asked me to come home. I had seen by now what life was like for kids who had nowhere to go and no way to make ends meet. So, I relented and went back to the condo in Tustin. My great sojourn in the land of freedom had come to an end.

Nothing at home had changed. The old Pakistani man was still renting my bedroom, meaning I was back on the living-room couch. I had to apologise to Mother and Dung for my disrespectful behaviour, and they let me know in no uncertain terms what they thought of me. It was humiliating and depressing. Naturally, they didn't even consider apologising to me, because they didn't think they'd done anything wrong. They needed the extra money that renting out the room would bring in, and if that was what had to be done, then I had no choice but to put up with it.

Something about this didn't seem right to me at the time; however, I should point out that it is still a very common practice for Asian families to rent out rooms to as many people as can reasonably be squeezed into one house or apartment. They can make a lot of money this way, and then they simply buy another apartment with the proceeds and start renting that out to maximum capacity as well. But both Mother and Dung were also working full-time jobs that paid well, and yet they seemed to have nothing to show for it. Where was their money going?

Mother's dirty little secret was gambling. She had a thing for a Vietnamese game that's sort of a cross between Memory and the Chinese game of mah-jong. She regularly met her friends on weekends to play at their houses. And she started to go to Las Vegas as often as she could. On top of that, when California allowed legal gambling, many casinos were built. Now she could play cards every day after work, and gambling became a form of daily entertainment. Within a year, she would have to give up the condo to pay her gambling debts. Her American dream would be ruined by a vice she could not control. Little did I know that this fire had been raging within her for years, even before we left Vietnam. She'd been borrowing money from friends and family to pay off her debts back in the days when she was selling jewellery in Saigon. It's probably better that I didn't learn this until later, because I would not have understood that she couldn't help herself.

It seemed to me that there were a lot of things my mother couldn't help: she couldn't help it that she left Hanh and me to fend for ourselves, or that she had done this to me again in Huu Dinh when she was forced to find work in Saigon; she couldn't help it that she wasn't able to show how much she loved me; she couldn't help it that she herself had been damaged beyond repair, even before I was born.

But these are the kinds of things that only a grown woman has the emotional resources to understand, and even then it's a challenge. A woman's relationship with her mother is probably the most important one she will ever have, in terms of setting the tone for future relationships with other women, with her daughters and especially with herself. Only now, at the age of forty, am I beginning to be able to forgive my mother for those things she couldn't help, and – infinitely more difficult – those things I think she could.

One of the consequences of running away was that I had to take three months of make-up classes to cover the schoolwork I had missed. I put up with this like I put up with sleeping on the couch: it was a necessary evil, a means to an end. By now, I had set my sights on getting out of the house legally, officially and permanently. I was seventeen years old and dying to be out from under the thumb of my mother. Ever since I was in the ninth grade, I had had a dream of becoming an accountant. I enjoyed maths at school and thought that this would be an interesting way to use my skills. Now, however, I gave up this dream, as higher education was not an option. I decided that the best way forward was for me to get an easy office job working as a secretary or administrative assistant, or a secure job in the government, so that I could earn my own money and be independent. The only other way I could think of to get out was through marriage. So, I also began to meet and date men instead of boys.

First, there was T, an engineer at a large firm in San Jose. I met him through one of my aunt's boyfriends. San Jose was a good six hours from LA, but he used to drive down to see me every other weekend. In return, I would cook him a big dinner, and then he would take me out on the town. T was much older than I was and a great deal more sophisticated. He introduced me to ballroom dancing and seduced me with his passionate nature and charming ways. He used to whisper that I had pretty breasts while we were making love, and his breath in my ear turned me on.

Then there was G, a twenty-five-year-old mechanic for a rental car company. G was Thai, not Vietnamese, but that didn't make a huge difference. The only problem was that I started seeing him while I was still seeing T, and once T found out, he dumped me. I was still very young and foolish, and really had no idea what I was doing. T would have made an excellent husband, but I was too blind to see it.

Nevertheless, G and I had fun. He enjoyed taking me to a nice Thai restaurant near the pier in Long Beach, where I especially enjoyed the fish and lobster dishes. He was also no slouch as a cook himself. His speciality was chicken with peanut sauce – delicious. After a few weeks, I discovered that G already had a girlfriend, but this made no great difference to me. We kept seeing each other anyway. I was not really thinking about the future; I was thinking about how good he made me feel.

Then, I met N.

N was one of seven children. He and his family had fled Vietnam around the same time as Mother and I. They had gone to Paris, where they opened a Vietnamese restaurant in the 11th arrondissement. I met him while he was in California on vacation, visiting some of his relatives who also happened to be my relatives. My phantom step-grandfather, Thanh – whom I barely knew, but who had affected my life in so many ways – was his grandfather. Although there was no blood between us, he and I were technically cousins. This was apparently a good thing, as marrying him would mean strengthening the bond between his wealthy family and my poor one.

But I wasn't quite ready to take the plunge. When he and I started dating, I was still in the middle of my senior year, or twelfth grade, and I had yet to graduate. Also, there was the matter of him not being able to work legally in the US. There were a lot of factors to consider, so things would have to move at their own pace.

Meanwhile, my English had finally improved to the point where I had the confidence to get a job. I started working at a Sizzler franchise across the street from Tustin High. It was hard on my feet, and hard in other ways, too. We offered an all-you-can-eat shrimp special, and it was my job to go around refilling people's plates. This, combined with my height of five feet two inches, earned me the nickname 'Shrimp Lady'. But despite the hard work and my nickname, I loved earning my own pay. When I got my first cheque, I cashed it immediately and spent every penny of it on flowers for myself. My love for flowers had never abated, even though it had almost been the end of me that long-ago day when I had fallen into the Mekong reaching for a water lily.

In 1986, I graduated from high school with a final grade point average (GPA) of 3.5; the highest was 4.0. I was happy with this, although Mother wasn't – she was disappointed that I had not earned honours. But considering the difficulties I had had in the last few years, especially with English as a second language, I was rather proud of myself. (In fact, it took me ten years of living in America before I could speak English with a high degree of fluency.) I was now an American high-school graduate, which was the highest level of education any woman in my immediate family had ever achieved. My mother, grandmother and half-aunts all attended the ceremony. They were not generous with their praise, but I could tell nonetheless that they were impressed and proud. I was pleased that I had made it through after all the bewilderment of the past years. As a tradition in America, there was a graduation prom for seniors but I decided not to attend, as even then I still felt very much an outsider.

After graduation, N began coming to visit me as often as he could, frequently spending the night at our house. Maybe at first I had had a bit of a crush on him, but this soon passed and at times I felt slightly uneasy being in his company. However, I continued to see him. I felt sorry for him, particularly because he could not stay and work in the US. He pleaded with me to help him and I was too young, weak and naive to say no. I felt that he put a lot of pressure on me and there didn't seem to be anyone I could turn to for help. I trusted no one, not even my mother, who was deeply involved in her gambling at the time.

One day, N told me that he wanted to stay in the US with me. He said that he wanted to take me away from my mother and claimed that he would take care of me like a princess. But before he could do that, he had to earn his 'green card', or permanent resident status. Before he could do that, he had to marry me. And even before he could do *that*, I had to finalise the journey I had begun in 1979 by getting on that fishing boat in My Tho: I had to become a US citizen.

Up to that time, getting my citizenship had not carried much importance. I thought of it as a bureaucratic formality that I would eventually have to go through, something like getting a California driver's licence. But sitting in the LA County Courthouse prior to the swearing-in ceremony, looking at the shining faces of the other immigrants all around me – each and every one of whom was realising a huge ambition in their lives – it hit me how far I had come, and I became overwhelmed with emotion.

Before the ceremony began, they played Neil Diamond's 'Coming to America'. I found myself deeply touched by the simplicity and strong message of the lyrics.

When it was over, I walked out into the bright California sunshine and looked around me. Was it my imagination, or did everything seem a little different? Had my feelings about America changed now that I really belonged here? Maybe, maybe not. But I was suddenly very glad I had gone through with it.

Little by little, so gradually I'd hardly noticed it, I had started to become a whole new person. It had begun the day I left Huu Dinh and then got on that accursed boat. Now, the change was complete, as I had also taken the opportunity to officially change my name. Dung Nguyen, the little girl who had left Vietnam on that boat, was dead. She had been replaced by Juliet Lac – someone who was not quite Vietnamese, not quite American, never completely comfortable or happy, and never sure why.

During the ceremony, we were reminded of all the soldiers who had fought and died for the cause of American freedom. I thought of my father, who had also fought and died – not for the same flag but for the same ideals. I wondered what he would have thought of me that day as I put my hand over my heart and recited the Pledge of Allegiance. I wondered if maybe he was watching me from the other side, if he was sorry for all the emotional trauma he had put us through, and if he understood now how he had let us down. I was shocked in that moment to realise that it was still important that my father be proud of me, and I hoped that he was.

And then I thought of my little sister, Hanh. It had been ten years since she'd died. I had allowed myself to think of her only rarely since then, because with her loss a part of me had been closed off for ever. But now I let myself think, just for a moment, about all I had been through since she'd left me – the desperation of living in defeat under the Communists; the dark and lonely nights in Huu Dinh; the voyage across the South China Sea and the loss of all those poor souls, especially the young pregnant woman; and the hell of the refugee camp in Malaysia. I wondered, if she had been with me, whether she would have survived. Maybe it was better that she had died young rather than go through all that. Maybe, because of her sweetness and innocence, she had been spared a life of suffering by whatever spiteful, whimsical gods rule this chaotic earth.

But I still believed then, as I believe today, that life is a sacred gift. I began to believe that Hanh had not been spared anything: that was the wrong way to look at it. Rather, she had chosen to leave me when she did so that I would have a companion to watch over me and help me through all those dark moments ahead. It wasn't down to luck that I had survived so far; it was Hanh.

Why did I think this? Because I had a sudden vivid memory of how she and I used to sit in the window and watch the people go by in the street below, and especially how we had watched in silence as my father walked away from us for the last time, without so much as a wave in our direction. There was only one little girl in the window now – me. But I didn't see an empty space where she had been. I could still sense Hanh's presence next to me. She would always be next to me, no matter what happened. She had not abandoned me. It was I who had abandoned her, by walling off my heart.

I was an American now, whatever that meant. I had a new perspective on life, a new way of looking at things. From now on, I vowed, I would live life as if I meant it. I was just nineteen and about to embark on my real life's purpose, whatever that would happen to be. I hadn't found it yet – in fact, I hadn't even really begun looking. But the day I became an American was the day things changed for me. It was the day I took the first steps on my real life's path – not the path the Communists, or my mother, or Thuy Tinh had chosen for me, but a path of my own choosing and a life of my own design.

I swore then and there, on the courthouse steps, that I would make Hanh proud of me.

And then I stepped down onto the pavement.

10

Marriage

The day before I was to get married to N, I had a minor breakdown. Deep down inside me, I was terrified about the prospect of marriage, especially to a man I was unsure of. It was as if some part of me was trying to warn the rest of me about the kind of future I faced if I went ahead and tied the knot with him.

I was having two completely different sets of thoughts about the situation. One was that marrying him seemed like a good, practical idea. It would allow me to get away from my mother, and I would have my own male protector and breadwinner. This was my practical side, the side that was worried only about survival. But to another part of me – to my heart – it just felt wrong. I didn't love him. Sometimes, I didn't even like him very much and felt manipulated by him.

But listening to my heart was something I had never been encouraged to do. In fact, it was a luxury that I had never been able to afford. When you are a war baby, as I am, you get used to walling yourself off from the outside world, because it is a very dangerous place, and part of you shuts down inside, too. You just try to make it through each day without getting hurt, and you take whatever you can get, when you can get it. This strategy had served me well so far. After all, I was still alive, wasn't I? But it would be years later before I could examine this strategy and realise that it was actually causing me a lot of trouble in my relationships, as well as in just about every other area of my life. This way of thinking led me to keep away from everyone and close them out in the cold. This is just one more example of how the real cost of war is still being exacted from its victims years after the war itself has ended. Fighting between the North and South had stopped in Vietnam, but it had sparked another war deep within myself. I have not heard any other Vietnamese people say this about themselves – admitting vulnerability would be looked down upon in our culture – but I would venture to guess that if they took a moment to look really deep inside their own hearts, they would realise that they feel much the same.

The day of this breakdown was a bad one for me. I didn't even understand that there was a battle raging deep inside me. I knew something wasn't right, but I had no idea what it was. I burst into tears and locked myself in the bathroom, vowing not to go through with the ceremony. My mother's reaction was typical – she ignored me. But N's uncle, to whom I had never felt particularly close, surprised us all by saying that if I didn't feel ready, then I should take some time to think about it.

Of course, with all those people waiting for me to make up my mind, this kind-hearted gesture did little to ease the real pressure. Looking back now, I can see that my real goal was not to marry N or anyone else. It was to get out and be independent. I knew that if I had to live one more year at home, I would go crazy. It was not so much about getting away from my mother as about being free. So, as they say in America, I jumped out of the frying pan and into the fire.

There was a great deal of additional pressure coming from N himself. He, like me, seemed to have few, if any, romantic notions about our union. For him, it appeared to be a practical matter – he wanted to live in the US and get a green card. There were several reasons for this, but the main one was that it was much easier to get a high-paying job in America than it was in France. N had big ambitions. He saw himself as a high-flying businessman, a wheeler-dealer. He had also hired a lawyer, a friend of his aunt's, to help push through the paperwork he would need to stay in the country. I believed that if I refused to go through with the wedding, his entire life would be thrown into chaos, his dreams for the future would be shot down in flames, and it would all be my fault. I didn't like this kind of responsibility, but since I had my own selfish reasons for wanting the wedding, I finally decided to ignore my heart and do the practical thing. As is always the case when we ignore that which is most important to us, it was a move I would regret for the rest of my life.

The next day, in a brusque civil ceremony that made my citizenship ceremony seem like a royal pageant, we became man and wife. It was a miserable ten minutes for me. None of our family was there and afterwards there was no honeymoon.

Along with everything else I was feeling, it bothered me that I didn't have a traditional white-gown ceremony like American brides did. I didn't mourn the lack of a traditional Vietnamese wedding, because I had never seen one. I was American enough now to want the same things that other girls had, but the fairytale white wedding wasn't going to happen for me.

Ironically, given my reasons for going through with the marriage, for the first month after the wedding N and I were forced to live in my mother's condo in Tustin because we did not yet have any money of our own. At least we didn't have to sleep on the couch – that really would have been the final insult. The Pakistani man was told to move out, and I reclaimed the bedroom that had been the scene of my brief happiness. But now I had acquired a husband who would share it with me.

Not only was N firmly ensconced in my bedroom, he also felt perfectly entitled to boss me around and speak to me as he pleased. Who was going to contradict him? He was my husband. By our Vietnamese rules, that meant he was running the show, while I was there only to follow orders. He even went so far as to take my car and trade it in for a pickup truck without asking my opinion on the matter, let alone my permission.

But I did not see myself as being a humble Vietnamese housewife. I had not forgotten my goal of making something of myself, even though I still wasn't sure what that something would be. I was determined to get a job, so I began working for a temp agency, where I earned up to nine dollars an hour for clerical and secretarial work. I liked working as a temp, as it meant that my work schedule was quite flexible. Of course, our financial situation dictated that this wasn't actually a choice but a necessity. I had to go to work, but I welcomed the challenge and the rewards it brought.

N's English was not as good as mine, so the best job he was able to find was as a lab technician at a Japanese-owned film-processing company for six dollars an hour. He and I made a combined gross income of $30,000 a year. This was not enough to live in any kind of style, but it was enough to start saving money in dribs and drabs, provided we skimped on just about everything – including rent. The one benefit of living with Mother was that she didn't charge us anything. But I was determined that we were going to move out. So, as soon as we were able, we left the condo in Tustin and moved to Garden Grove, where we shared an apartment with a young Chinese couple and their five-year-old daughter.

I also took the next step on my path to fulfilment and rekindled one of my dreams – I enrolled in night school at Santa Ana College, where I studied accounting. I was proud of myself for taking this step towards a better life. What, after all, was the point of surviving everything I had been through, I often asked myself, if I wasn't going to accomplish something worthwhile? So I threw myself into my work and my studies, and at night I came home, exhausted, to our overcrowded apartment, threw myself into bed and submitted to N's gropings, pantings and thrustings. Our sex life was never enjoyable for me, but since my reasons for marrying him had nothing to do with romance, I wasn't surprised or even particularly disappointed by this. I just regarded it as the price I had to pay for my eventual freedom.

Now, at the age of forty, I shake my head at the stupidity of my teenage self. I wish I could reach back in time, grab the younger me by the shoulders and give her a good shake. 'Wake up!' I would say. 'Don't do things for selfish reasons! Think about the long-term consequences! And listen to your heart!'

But soon my plans were changed drastically – not by outside forces, but by inner ones. Specifically, a very small inner force – a baby. Within a month of our marriage, I became pregnant.

Typically, I had given no thought to the consequences of my actions. N and I had been having sex without birth control, and I had left it up to chance to determine what would happen. Still only nineteen years old, I was devastated and terrified by my pregnancy. In many ways, as is common among survivors of all types of catastrophic events, I was frozen at the age I was when those things happened. At nineteen, I was still that little girl hiding from the missiles that flew overhead, wetting her pants with fear. I was a baby having a baby, and I was in no way ready to become a mother.

While re-reading this manuscript, I realise that I might come across to some as the kind of person who would feel sorry for herself whatever happened. And I know also that people who think this way tend to be less successful and happy in their lives, because in their own minds they are always helpless victims. But in my defence, I would argue that I never wanted to be this way, and I did have some serious emotional problems that were crying out to be dealt with. No one around me offered any help, but then again nor did I ask for any. I can see now that I should have sought counselling, but I was Vietnamese enough to feel that it was shameful to admit to weakness or vulnerability, so I just carried on.

I kept working until my sixth month, when I gained a great deal of weight all at once. Then, to my despair, not only did my condition force me to quit my temp job, but I had to quit night school as well. I resigned myself to staying home and getting fatter, but what was worse, I was forced to submit to the humiliation of applying for Medicare at the local welfare office. I was glad it was available, since it meant I could see almost any doctor for free, as well as get medicine for myself and the baby. But, all the same, it was a sign that we were poor, and I hated having to do it.

This is another cultural trait. Not everyone feels the way we Vietnamese do about government handouts. In neither America nor France do you see block after block of decrepit Vietnamese neighbourhoods, the residents content to live in poverty while expecting everyone else in the world to help them out. This is not our way. Then, as now, I didn't want to have to rely on anyone else to get by.

For N, meanwhile, life went on as normal. He was at work most of the day and late into the night. When he came home, he jumped right into bed and slept straight through until he had to wake up and get ready to go to work again. And I rarely saw my mother during the course of my pregnancy, as she was busy with her own life.

On 4 February 1987, I began to experience severe abdominal pain. I called N at work, and he rushed home and drove me to hospital. They admitted me right away and showed me to a room. I put on a gown and lay down on the bed. Then I began to practise some relaxation techniques. The pains eased somewhat, but every thirty minutes they returned with a vengeance. It was unlike anything I had ever experienced. I felt like I was being tortured. I swore up and down that I would never, ever let N put a hand on me again. I had found our sex life unpleasant, and now this was the end result? I could easily give up sex for the rest of my life if this was how things were going to turn out.

Finally, the doctor showed up. He felt my belly, frowned and said that the baby was still lying with its head to the side. It needed to turn round so the head was facing down. It was going to be a while longer, he said. I could only stare at him in dumb silence. *Why don't you just cut me open now and take it out?* I wanted to ask. But my respect for the medical profession was so great that it was akin to fear; I would never think of questioning a doctor's wisdom.

The doctor went away, and N told me that, as the baby wasn't coming yet, he was going back to work. I was so disenchanted with him by this point that, already, less than a year into our marriage, I preferred lying alone in pain to having him in the same room with me.

N left, and the pain returned, worse than ever. I grabbed the sides of the bed and tried not to scream. Showing outward signs of pain was a weakness; my people prized stoicism and compliance above all else, especially in times such as this. I did not want to let them down, even though no one was in the room with me.

This highlighted another cultural difference, and sometimes the contrast can seem humorous. Around this time, a very large Mexican woman in the late stages of labour was wheeled in. She had no qualms whatsoever about letting the world know how she felt. Every time her labour pains struck, she let out a scream that could have wakened my ancestors on the other side of the world. The more she screamed, the more I tried to hold my pain in and the harder I gripped the sides of the bed. It seems funny now but, at the time, I was in hell.

This went on all night. N showed up again around noon the next day. I was so mad at him by then that I told him to get lost, that I never wanted to see him again. After a little while, he left for work again, and I was alone once more.

The pain kept coming and coming and coming. A nurse felt my belly and told me that I was almost there. I asked for some painkillers, and she told me she would go and ask the doctor, but she never came back.

Time began to blur and the pains started to come more quickly. Finally, around five that evening, more than twenty-four hours after the pain had begun, the nurse began to clean me up in preparation for giving birth. I started to push on my own, but they told me to wait until the doctor came. When he finally got around to showing up, he took his time washing his hands and putting his gloves on. Then he informed me that I was ready to start pushing.

I knew that, I thought.

I felt cold steel. The doctor told me he had to make an incision called an episiotomy in my pelvic floor, because my vagina was too small for the baby's head. I couldn't have cared less about this, and in fact I didn't even feel it, so great was my pain now.

Finally, the doctor announced that he could see the baby's head coming. Then, suddenly, it was out.

'It's a boy!' he said.

I looked up to see the doctor holding the baby upside down.

'Why isn't it moving?' I asked fearfully.

Instead of replying, he gave my son a smack on his bottom. This woke him up, and he began to wail. I was so exhausted that I barely had time to feel relieved before I fell asleep and they took my baby away to clean him up.

A few hours later, they brought the baby back to me. I examined him from head to toe, as all mothers do. I was amused to see that he was very hairy – not only on his head, but also on his back.

I spent a restless and uncomfortable night trying to nurse him and get comfortable at the same time. Now the episiotomy had become intensely painful, and I wasn't happy no matter what position I was in. To make matters worse, the baby didn't want to nurse. He fussed at the nipple and kept biting me, which – even though he was toothless – was extremely painful.

N's mother, whom I had never met before, had flown in from Paris for the big event. She and my mother came to the hospital and cooed over the baby. N himself finally showed up again and announced that he had decided to name the baby Sonny, after a character on his favourite TV show, *Miami Vice*. This caught me by surprise. I had been pushing for Kevin or Michael, but in the end I was not consulted; he already had the birth certificate in hand. Naturally, I was too tired and sore to argue.

The next day, I was released from the hospital. N, Sonny and I went back to the apartment we shared with the Chinese couple and their five-year-old daughter. They had now rented out the third bedroom to yet another couple, with whom we were to share a bathroom. These people didn't have any children yet, but this now meant that there were six adults and two kids in a three-bedroom place.

I was in a lot of pain from the incision, and Sonny still wasn't nursing well. To make matters worse, he cried constantly – especially late at night. To his credit, N was patient with him. He held him, fed him and did his best to soothe him during those late-night hours, so that I could get a little bit of sleep. In true Vietnamese fashion, he was delighted to have had a son.

But, for the most part, I was left alone with the baby. I was in a state of constant exhaustion. It's hard enough when a newborn is fussy or colicky, but we were crammed into this tiny apartment with all these people, and the new couple complained whenever the baby's cries disturbed them. This only added to the immense pressure, anxiety and frustration that I was feeling.

I began to have disturbing thoughts, thoughts so evil I couldn't even believe they were coming out of my own head. When Sonny simply wouldn't stop his screaming, I used to fantasise about running over him with a car to make him shut up. Then I would feel horrified at myself for even thinking such a thing. This happened over and over. It was a vicious cycle that seemed totally beyond my control. Of course, I would never have actually done such a thing. But I did do something that I am very ashamed of today – I put a pillow over my baby to muffle the sound of his cries. I didn't do it to hurt him. I did it so that I could sleep. It worked – I finally got a few hours of much-needed rest. But then, when I woke, I was horrified at what I had done. Hurriedly I took the pillow away, fearing the worst. He was sleeping peacefully, unharmed. I was overwhelmed with relief . . . but then I did it again and again and again.

Today, I know that I was suffering all the symptoms of post-natal depression. At its worst, this is a condition that can lead women to do things to their children that the rest of us would never imagine, not in our worst nightmares. Of course, those are extreme examples. Milder forms of post-natal depression are very common among women and can show up long after the baby is born – sometimes years later – making it harder to diagnose. There are various causes. Sometimes it's hormonal.

Other times it's due to exhaustion, lack of proper nutrition or lack of support in the home. It might be something as simple as difficulty in nursing, as I experienced. Often the natural fears and anxieties that one feels at being a first-time parent are blown up and magnified. It is very important for women who feel that they may be experiencing these symptoms, also called 'baby blues', to talk to a doctor, nurse or counsellor about it.

I wish now that I'd had someone to turn to. But I was once again stymied by the twin obstacles of the Vietnamese tendency to hide one's problems and the lack of any kind of familial support. I had to learn about post-natal depression from the same source that had taught me about sex: the television.

My depression got worse and worse. I knew I had to do something, and so I hit upon the idea of getting out of that sardine can of an apartment and into somewhere more comfortable. We couldn't afford to do this on our own, but I convinced N to come with me to the welfare office, where we applied for housing assistance. There was a long list of people ahead of us, but because of our new baby, we only had to wait a month. Then we were able to move into a rent-subsidised two-bedroom apartment in Garden Grove. It felt like moving into a palace. Sonny had room to breathe, and so did I.

But things did not get easier for me in other ways. N was still out at work much of the time, and taking care of the apartment was solely my responsibility. This meant cooking, cleaning, doing laundry and even yard work, in addition to caring for the baby – who was still fussy. I had given up nursing Sonny after one month, because neither he nor I were taking to it very well. Yet I felt guilty about this decision. I knew that it was healthier to breast-feed children than bottle-feed them, but we just couldn't make it work.

About this time, I took Sonny to Paris for three weeks to visit N's family. His parents, brothers and sisters were delighted to look after him, and for the first time in three months I was able to sleep and rest. It was like heaven. Returning home again felt like just the opposite.

Three months after our visit to France, when Sonny was six months old, I had had enough. I was depressed again, still tired, still unsatisfied and convinced that I would never do a good job as a mother. Ninety-five per cent of the time, I was left alone to care for my child. N loved his son, but he had no sense of how much work it was to raise him, and he did what he pleased, constantly working late, and, I suspected, going out with his mates. In my despair, I remembered how happy his family had been to have Sonny with them. Even Sonny himself had seemed happier there, because everyone around him was so much more relaxed. He wasn't alone with me all the time, with my worries, fears and anxieties. It hurt me deeply to admit it, but I saw that my baby had been happier around his father's family than he was around his own mother. And, worst of all, I was still having those horrifying fantasies of hurting my baby. Every day, I was convinced that I was one step closer to enacting the blood-chilling scenario that had been playing over and over in my mind: running Sonny over with the car. What was wrong with me? Was I crazy? Was I a criminal? I desperately needed help before something awful happened, and it felt like time was running out.

I would have liked to have been able to turn to my own mother for help, but unfortunately she was no good with children – she liked holding them for a few minutes, but then she passed them on to someone else, and that was it. I felt that asking her for assistance was out of the question and, apart from her, there was no one else.

I thought it over and told N what I was thinking: I wanted to send Sonny to Paris, to stay with his family there. It would just be for a little while, until I was better able to care for him, until we had more money. Of course, I never said anything about my awful secret fantasies. He would not have understood. Few people do, unless they have experienced it themselves.

This was an extremely difficult decision for me. It meant admitting failure as a mother, and the guilt was insurmountable, but I was really worried by this time about what Sonny's life would be like if he was stuck with me.

N called his parents and asked them what they thought about my suggestion. They were overjoyed, as I had suspected they would be. The decision was made. Sonny and I went back to Paris, but this time, I stayed only a few days. When I left, I was alone, and Sonny had a new home.

It is impossible for me to explain the sense of emptiness and loss I felt when I got on the plane to go back to California without my little boy. The child in me had eagerly anticipated the freedom that would come from not having to care for him any more. But the woman in me was broken-hearted. The guilt was unbearable. Only the knowledge that I had probably saved Sonny's life by giving him up made me feel a little bit better. But even that was nothing in comparison to the fact that the person I was saving him from was myself. I felt like a failure not just as a mother but also as a human being.

Once, my mother had had to surrender me to the waves of the South China Sea in the hope that I would survive the storm and wash up safe on shore. It was a gamble that had paid off. Now, a generation later, I had to surrender my own child in a different way, to protect him from a different kind of storm. I could only pray that he too would find safe shelter from the kind of agony that this life can bring. I had known nothing but pain and turmoil so far. Please, I prayed – to God, to Thuy Tinh, to whoever was listening – let Sonny be spared those things. Let him find some peace and happiness. Let him live and be free; let him not forget his mother even if he never sees me again; let him know always that I did what I did because I love him.

In early February of 1988, N and I decided to go to France to visit Sonny. I felt such a strange mixture of emotions at the prospect of seeing my baby again – joy, of course, but also fear. What if he didn't remember me? How would N's family treat me? Would I plunge once again into despair and guilt after coming home?

For I knew, ahead of time, that Sonny would not be coming back with me, even though I had a good job now. For one thing, he would scarcely have a home to come to. N and I saw each other so infrequently that I had almost forgotten we were married. And for another, I was still unsure whether I had conquered the demons in my heart that made me want to hurt my baby. My mother love outweighed my mother guilt. If Sonny was safer in Paris, then that was where he would stay.

When we arrived in Paris, N's family closed their restaurant for the night to have a party. The celebration was in honour of my son's first birthday. For me, it was a bittersweet occasion. I tried many times to get him to come to me, but after almost six months apart, Sonny had largely forgotten who I was. Also, although I could hardly believe this, there was already a language barrier between us. N's family spoke to Sonny only in French, a language I had no understanding of, and he didn't seem to remember any Vietnamese. This saddened me greatly, but there was no one to whom I could talk about it.

And hanging in the air between N's mother and me was an unspoken understanding – Sonny was lost to me for ever. I had given him up once, and that meant he was no longer mine. No doubt she considered me an unfit mother. I had never told anyone about my secret desire to hurt my child, but sometimes I still wonder if his mother knew anyway. Women are intuitive about certain things. There is a great deal they don't need to be told. I had mostly recovered from my post-natal depression by now, but even I could see that Sonny really was happy in Paris – much more so than he ever could have been in California. The reason was very simple: in Paris, he would have a family of at least eight people around him, all of whom would care for him and love him dearly.

I, on the other hand, couldn't stand Paris. I found it grey, dirty and cold, and the pavements were covered in dog excrement. This is something I will never understand – and it's telling that even someone who grew up in a developing country, with no laws or regulations governing the disposal of rubbish or the preparation of food, still managed to be appalled by the situation.

While I was in Paris, to distract myself from the pain I was feeling about Sonny, I went to a very expensive hair salon. A man named Franck, who was about my age, spent two hours pampering me and giving me the latest style. When I came out, I really looked like a movie star – and I have never considered myself to be particularly attractive.

The haircut was one bright spot in an otherwise difficult trip, and the best part was that it lasted until long after our return home. One day, soon after we came back, I was driving myself to work at the courthouse when a handsome young man in the next car gave me his business card and asked if I would call him. Such a thing had never happened to me before, and I was fairly sure it never would again. But it helped boost one tiny corner of my always-sagging but never-completely-collapsed sense of who I was.

11

Depression

I had never thought for a moment that life without Sonny was going to be the same as life before N, before marriage, before pregnancy. I was not delusional enough to believe that I could undo anything that had already happened to me. I'd learned enough at the school of hard knocks to understand that what's done is done and there's no use lamenting it. I was prepared to deal with any consequence, emotional or otherwise, that might have come about as a result of giving away my own child. But the one thing I was unprepared for was feeling nothing. Yet this is exactly the feeling that consumed me after leaving Sonny in Paris following his first birthday: the feeling of nothingness.

Every waking moment felt completely empty. I had no thoughts, no dreams, no emotions. I felt like an empty shell. It wasn't just good feelings that escaped me. The same was true of bad ones as well. I couldn't even bring myself to be annoyed at N any more. I simply felt nothing. When I thought of my son, or looked at pictures of him, I searched myself for a twinge of maternal emotion. Maybe it was there. But it was buried so deep under layers of denial that it might as well not have existed at all.

I felt like a walking dead woman.

Yet somewhere inside me, the ambition to succeed lay dormant. Like the famous brine shrimp of the Mojave Desert, who live asleep under the salt flats for years until the rains come again (these are actually the famous 'Sea Monkeys' that kids used to be able to order through comic books in the 1970s and 1980s), it began to re-emerge. I don't know what forces caused this to happen in me. Maybe it was my own resilience and toughness – for as much as the events of my life had scarred me up to this point, they had also made me so strong as to be practically bulletproof. Quite possibly I was so distraught about the loss of my baby that I had to focus on something – anything – else. Or maybe it was Hanh, gently reminding me from the spirit world why I was here. I like to think that she and my father – who, now that he was a spirit too, could see all the wrong he'd done to us and was repentant for it – were still rooting for me from the Other Side.

I did not have such thoughts then, however. At the time, I could barely see past the end of my own nose. Such is the awful power of depression.

I enrolled once again at Santa Ana College as an accounting major, hoping to pick up where I had left off before falling pregnant. But when I began my classes, I was disappointed beyond words to find that I couldn't stay awake for more than a few minutes during lectures or while trying to read my textbooks. It was as if a switch had been turned off inside my head, and I found it impossible to continue with the course.

I had to give up any notion of being an accountant. That was the only bit of professional ambition I'd had left in me. Now, with that gone, I didn't know where to turn or what to think about. I became like a robot, just going through the motions of life. I registered with the temporary agency once again. One day here, another day there – it was the perfect kind of work for me. I didn't have to get attached to anything or anyone. I kept my head down, did whatever menial tasks were assigned and collected my pay cheque.

The one reliable thing about my life in those days was that time would pass without any help from me. The clock ticked whether I was asleep or awake. I took a strange comfort in this obvious fact, because I certainly couldn't depend on anything, or anyone, else. The days began to blur again. Weeks became months. Before I knew it, I had turned twenty-one. Nobody remembered my birthday – not N, not even my mother. I didn't feel sorry for myself, though. I didn't even care. If someone had thrown a party for me, I would have just sat in the corner and stared dumbly at the floor, so it was just as well that everyone forgot.

To make ends meet, N took a second job delivering copies of the *Orange County Register*. To do this, he had to get up at three in the morning. I used to get up with him and sit in the back of the truck – that damned truck he'd bought without even consulting me – and toss the papers onto people's doorsteps. We also delivered to apartment complexes, for which he had to get out and walk from door to door. We did this rain or shine, of course. But, as any American paperboy knows, rain makes things much more complicated. You have to put each paper in its own plastic bag, and if you're unprepared for the weather, you just get wet. You can't wait for the sun to come out again. People must have their papers on time or they complain bitterly. We needed the money too badly to risk unhappy customers. At least in southern California we didn't have to worry about snow.

One morning, long before dawn, we were delivering papers in an apartment complex when there came a thunderous downpour. I had no coat or umbrella with me. Neither did N. But as soon as it started raining, N suddenly developed a mysterious stomach ailment. He told me to finish the rest of the papers by myself and went back to the truck and sat in the cab, dry as a bone. I went on and dropped the papers off at each individual doorstep. I was mad at him, but not mad enough to say or do anything about it. I couldn't even bring myself to care that he was taking advantage of me.

At one particular apartment, I had just dropped the paper and was about to walk away when the door opened and a woman stood there, staring at me. It was still very early, and hardly anyone else was up. I was so surprised that all I could do was stare back at her.

We stood there for a long moment, regarding each other. She was a white woman, middle-aged, middle-class, warm and dry in her little place – which I did not begrudge her in the slightest.

If it's possible to tell anything about people by looking at them for only a few seconds, then she looked to me like someone who had worked hard to get to where she was in her life and was more or less content. I could tell by the expression on her face what she thought when she looked at me. Deep inside the older woman's eyes, she seemed to be the only person in the world who understood me. She alone seemed to feel my pain.

I was soaked to the skin, shivering, my hair hanging in my face – once again exposed to the elements, just as Mother and I had been on the deck of the overloaded fishing boat that brought us to Malaysia. What I saw in this woman's face was not mistrust or pity. It's not like whites and Asians weren't used to seeing each other on a daily basis everywhere in southern California. It was merely a moment in which two lives that otherwise have nothing in common crossed paths, and each of us found the contrast shocking.

Another more dramatic event was soon to follow. N and I sometimes had to deliver papers in the afternoon, too. I was walking down the stairs in another apartment complex, having delivered an armload of the *Register*, when I heard a rumbling sound, and the stairs began to shake. I tumbled down them and landed, hard, on the cement sidewalk. Soon the shaking subsided, and I made my way back to the truck. I was scared but unhurt. It was my first experience of an earthquake.

N drove us home, and when we got back to our apartment, he turned on the television and we watched in horror as footage of the devastation in San Francisco unfolded on the screen. What we had felt was a greatly watered-down version of the Loma Prieta Earthquake, the Quake of '89. It wasn't the Big One that Californians have been fearing for decades, but to those of us living in California then, it certainly seemed like it – and we didn't know if there was going to be a bigger one soon after.

As it turned out, there were many aftershocks, but none of them were as bad as that first tremor. And that was bad enough. Sixty-two people died, including six people on one street corner who were crushed by falling bricks, and many thousands more were injured or left homeless. The tremor also caused the collapse of the San Francisco–Oakland Bay Bridge. I was not used to earthquakes, but I was used to devastation and destruction, and the fact that this was happening so close to home bothered me. No place on earth, I realised – not even the great America – was safe from catastrophe.

It was at this point that our housing contract with the city's welfare department ended. That meant we either had to move out of our apartment or start paying the full rent on it ourselves. Since paying was out of the question, we had to move again. And once again, there was only one place for us to go where the rent was free: back to Mother's. If I had not been so emotionally frozen, I might have got upset about this. But at this point, you could have taken my hand and stuck it in a candle flame, and I would have just left it there until someone else came along and moved it out again.

I had been gone all of two years. Mother had another boyfriend by this time, and she spent a great deal of time at his place. That made things a touch easier, as it was a small place and three adults would have made it too crowded.

But I would have felt crowded by N even if he and I were the only two people in the Grand Canyon. By this time, he seemed more like a bossy roommate than a husband. It had been a long time since there was any physical intimacy between us. He had always been secretive – never showing me how much money he made at his job or how much he had in his bank account, never telling me where he was going or who he was going to be with, or when he was going to be home. I was expected to sit and wait for him – not to have any hopes or expectations of my own but to accept whatever he handed me and not to ask any questions.

I couldn't put up with this for ever, of course. Being downtrodden is not my true nature – it was only my current circumstance. I fought back verbally and found other little ways to subvert him as well. I tried to get under his skin when I felt it would bother him most. One day he and I were talking about something – I don't even remember what – when something I said pushed him over the edge, and we got into the biggest argument we had ever had. I was terrified as he screamed and shouted at me, and eventually I turned and left the apartment.

It was dark out. I walked and walked for hours, not caring where I was going, not sure where I belonged. When I got tired, I sat on a bench and waited for my energy to return. I might have used this time to reflect on my life thus far and to try to figure out how I had got into this situation, but I had no strength for that kind of thinking. I just sat there, as blank as a new canvas.

When I could get up again, I found a pay phone and called my mother to tell her what had happened. I might not always have been able to rely on her for emotional support, but she was, quite literally, the only person in the world I could turn to at that moment, and this time she came through for me.

Mother came in her boyfriend's car, picked me up and took me back to his apartment. Then she called N and ripped into him. I'd heard Mother talk trash before, but never like this. Then she went one step further. She called his parents and told them what had gone on. In our culture, which places such reliance on family and honour, this was almost as bad as calling the police. I have no idea what his family said to him about the incident, but I am sure they didn't let it pass without mention.

After this, I scarcely saw him at all. He did his thing, and I did mine. Occasionally we saw each other on weekends, but we did not exchange two words when we did. Our marriage, if it had ever really existed, was over in every way except by law.

I began to spend more time with my mother, and, at her urging and with her financial support, I enrolled in cosmetology school. Whatever dreams I had once had now seemed lost for ever. So, to beauty school I went. I learned all the arts of making women look good – hair, nails, facials, et cetera. I needed 1,600 hours of training to receive my certificate, and I worked at it diligently, learning as much as I could.

I learned something else, too – how to feel a little bit of physical satisfaction again.

L was cute, not drop-dead gorgeous but definitely attractive, and a neat, clean dresser – which has always been a must for me when it comes to men. We met at the beauty school. He was young, single and full of life. We exchanged shy glances at first. Then, one day when we were alone for a moment in a parking lot at a nearby restaurant, we kissed. That was all it took to open the floodgates once again. L took me back to his house, and we made love like I had never done before.

It was wonderful, ecstatic and deeply satisfying. He was an incredible lover. Underneath all the issues that had been smothering me for years, I was still a woman, and I still craved that deep connection with a man – that feeling that only a really skilled, attentive lover can give. And L was, without doubt, the best lover I have ever had. Needless to say, I had never felt that way about N. Even mentioning his name in the same breath as L is ludicrous. Was it wrong for me to break my marriage vows this way? Well, for one thing, N had been working such long hours that I hardly ever saw him, and some nights he didn't even come home. When I asked where he had been, he said that he had been at work because they were short of people on the night shift. Also, I had not allowed him to touch me for months or even years.

It was unfortunate, but then I realise now that I should never have married N in the first place. At the time, I just knew that I felt free. And, most importantly of all, I was beginning to feel alive again.

When I finished my beauty school training, Mother was pleased because she wanted to open a hair and skin-care salon, and I could now help her to run it. But to her disappointment, before I could take the certification exam I decided to switch careers and become a licensed massage therapist instead. The reason for this was simply that the money was better. Despite her disappointment, Mother once again agreed to finance my tuition, and when this course was completed, I got a job at a clinic in Newport. But I found the work hard-going physically and didn't see myself continuing with it for long. Also, there were a lot of men who asked for more than massages, and this atmosphere disturbed me.

So, early in 1991, I took my civil service exams, passed and was hired by the Traffic Department at the County Courthouse. Finally, I had something like a real job, one that offered benefits, stability, decent pay and the promise of eventual advancement.

The work itself was interesting, sometimes funny and sometimes highly aggravating, as is any job that involves dealing with the public. In the morning, I worked at the counter accepting payments and giving extensions to traffic violators. In the afternoon, I worked at my desk, issuing arrest warrants for those with misdemeanour charges who had failed to appear in court.

The general attitude of people in traffic court is that they will do anything possible to get out of paying their fine. This happened constantly. People didn't show up on the right day, they refused to pay, they didn't complete traffic school and they offered every excuse in the book: they were speeding because the freeway was empty and they could; they were speeding because they were late for work; they were speeding because they were late to pick up their kids; because their wife was having a baby . . . it went on and on. I heard every excuse there was. As southern California, like many other places in America, is a mishmash of people from every culture you can think of, many people didn't speak English, and so we had to have a variety of translators on hand.

But despite the chaos, I liked my job, and it was there that I made the first real friend I'd had in a long time: Sara. She was a woman about my age, tall and slender with long hair – but I felt no jealousy towards her for having the body type I'd always wanted. I was slowly learning to be more accepting of myself. Sara was always calm, always patient with people, and I loved being around her. We frequently spent our lunch hours together and shared stories of our lives. She invited me to her place and introduced me to her live-in boyfriend, who was a portrait photographer. She knew about my troubles with my marriage and I knew about difficulties she was also having in her life. Sara also introduced me to her parents, her older brother and her two younger sisters. Both of her sisters were at university, one studying civil engineering and the other studying economics in San Diego. I frequently went to see Sara at her place at the weekends, and we would cook and go out to see movies together. We both enjoyed and appreciated each other's company. Sara was a friend who never criticised me for being who I am and what I am, even when I made mistakes, and we remain friends today.

12

One Step Forward, Two Steps Back

In 1992, I found a better-paying job with the City Public Library system. There I worked as a clerk, checking books in and out, issuing lender cards and helping to organise special ethnic events for children in the community. I particularly enjoyed this last part of my job because there were so many Vietnamese and Chinese children in the neighbourhood. One of my duties was to help organise the Tet, or New Year, Festival, as well as the Moon Festival.

The Moon Festival is based on an ancient legend about gods and goddesses. Like many Chinese legends, it's a morality tale that carries with it the lessons of fidelity to one's parents and spouse, as well as other virtues. The Chinese and Vietnamese people believe that Chang Er and her husband Hou Yi, who were both divine, had been made mortal as a punishment, but Chang Er drank an elixir that made her immortal and flew up to the moon, where she has lived alone ever since. Our children are taught that if you look closely during the full moon in the eighth month, you can see her dancing there today.

This legend is only one part of the Moon Festival. It also involves folk dancing, beauty and talent pageants, martial arts exhibitions, dragon dancing, firecrackers, drumming and traditional Vietnamese entertainers. The children will put on their ao dai and give concerts for their beaming parents and grandparents. In some communities, the Moon Festival also includes more American-style activities, such as amusement park-style games and rides.

Seeing how excited the children became, and how much they liked eating moon cakes, a traditional dessert, reminded me of what it was like to be a little girl in Vietnam. During the Moon Festival back home, I wore ao dai made by my mother and joined the other children parading on the streets, singing with lanterns of different shapes and colours in our hands. There was also a dragon dance with Ong Dia (Lord Earth), who danced around the dragon urging it on. Ong Dia has a round happy smiling face like a moon cake. He represents prosperity and wealth on earth.

All that seemed a very long time ago to me now, even though I was still only a young woman myself. I felt as if I had lived a hundred lifetimes since leaving Vietnam. I particularly missed Sonny around the time of the Moon Festival and wondered what he would be doing now in Paris.

Around this time in 1992, the Rodney King trial concluded. This was the trial of four white police officers who had beaten a defenceless black man after he led them on a long and dangerous traffic chase during which the lives of many innocent people were needlessly put at risk. The officers denied the beating, but they had been caught on tape, and the tape was broadcast all over the world. America was horrified by what it saw. Many black leaders stood up at this time and said, 'See? We've been trying to tell you for years that this is how black people are treated by the system, but no one wanted to believe us. Here is the proof!'

Yet, somehow, despite the clear evidence of their guilt, the officers were allowed to go free. I never understood how this happened. Many others felt the same. Certain segments of the black community, notably the poorest of them, who lived downtown, erupted with rage. For them, this incident seemed to symbolise the centuries of oppression their ancestors had endured at the hands of Europeans, and especially the poverty they had suffered in America ever since the end of slavery. They expressed their anger in a puzzling fashion, however – they destroyed their own neighbourhoods. Of course, they hurt a lot of other people as well. Korean shop owners were attacked. They pulled white people randomly from cars and beat them as King had been beaten. One man, Reginald Denny, was pulled from his truck, beaten repeatedly, smashed in the head with a cinderblock and then had his wallet stolen. During this horrifying incident, one of his attackers actually stopped and waved at the news helicopter that was capturing the whole event.

All over the Los Angeles area, people were preparing for the worst. Nobody knew if the riots would spread, and if they did what the consequences would be. Americans are not used to civil disorder on this scale. It makes everyone very nervous. Eventually, things calmed down. But anyone who thinks that the trouble is over for good, even today, is fooling themselves. The riots are over, but the real problems are still there underneath the surface. Issues of racial tension, poverty, drug and alcohol abuse, violence and anger, to name just a few, haven't been dealt with at all.

Meanwhile, at the end of 1992, one of my aunts was getting married, and I was asked to be the maid of honour. I was flattered. I had thought that my cousin, Thao, who was taller and more beautiful than I, would be chosen. I came to learn that she had actually been asked first but had turned it down, because she had already been in two weddings that year. But I didn't even bother feeling hurt; I went ahead and did it anyway. Naturally, since N was related to this aunt – and because he was my husband – he was there, too. It was one of the few things we did together in public. Usually, whenever he went anywhere, I was not invited to go along with him.

I don't believe in fate, but that wedding turned out to be an auspicious occasion. That night, after we had come home, he and I did something we hadn't done in a long time: we had sex. It's funny how things happen sometimes. We weren't even drunk. It just happened. And a month later, something else happened as a result: I learned I was pregnant again.

I had never been to a professional therapist to deal with my earlier symptoms of depression, and I was afraid that another pregnancy could bring on the same feelings. So, I watched myself carefully to see if the same thing was going to happen to me again. But, to my relief, this pregnancy was an easy one. Our second boy, Kenny, was born in March of 1993. As is common with the birth of a second child, labour was much shorter this time – only two hours. I was profoundly grateful for this, remembering how difficult things had been the first time around.

I was also grateful for the fact that Kenny had a completely different personality from his brother. Instead of being fussy and colicky, he was calm and quiet, a good feeder and sleeper – a dream baby. How different things might have been if Sonny had been the same way! Nothing would have changed the fact that I was simply too young to become a mother the first time around, but maybe I would not have been plunged into the hell that I had been, with those terrifying, uncontrollable thoughts of hurting my baby.

After a brief period of rest at home, I went back to work. My schedule was regimented. I awoke at 5 a.m., fed Kenny, packed up his things, ate breakfast, showered and dressed, then drove him to daycare. Traffic was always horrible – in Los Angeles and the surrounding areas, if you have to drive anywhere, you can count on spending lots of time in your car every day. I worked until 5 p.m., then picked Kenny up, brought him home, fed him, washed him and put him to bed. Then I made dinner for myself, ate, cleaned up and fell asleep. I was always thoroughly exhausted by the end of the day. I saw little of N, who worked nights and slept all day. He loved both his sons very much, and he might assist me in feeding them during the evenings, but other than that I was on my own. On weekends, while he was again out of the house, I cleaned, mowed the lawn, did the laundry, went grocery shopping and did everything else that goes into running a household and caring for a baby. I was tired all the time. N rarely bothered to lift a finger to help with any of these other chores during those rare moments when he was home at all. Sometimes I wondered what he was up to, but I was really too tired – and too disenchanted with our marriage – to care.

Soon, I had another issue to worry about – money. One day when I was on my own in the house, I got a phone call from a debt-collection agency. To my horror, I learned that thousands of dollars of charges had been run up in my name without my knowledge. I was devastated, as I simply had no way to pay them.

I was beside myself with worry, and, then, to make matters worse, I found out I would have to cope with the situation on my own.

When Kenny was six months old, N was offered the opportunity to transfer to the French division of the Japanese film company he worked for. It meant more money, and so he took the job promptly – without consulting me, of course. Just like that, he was gone. I was left alone with Kenny and with the mountain of bills that had been run up. One time, N sent home a thousand dollars after I made many telephone calls telling his parents that Kenny and I needed his financial support. And that was it.

Once again, I had to call on all my resources just to stay afloat. I could depend on no one to help me with the day-to-day details of running a household, even a very small one, and caring for a child. There were a million things to be attended to, and I had to do every single one of them myself. I began to slip into depression again. Under the same set of circumstances, who wouldn't? It was horrible. I could feel myself going over the cliff, trying frantically to find some kind of handhold before I went, head over heels, back into the abyss I had just barely managed to crawl out of. But there was nothing for me to hang on to – nothing.

Incredibly, it was several months after his arrival in France that N finally got around to calling to check on me and his baby son. I was not glad to hear from him. In his absence, I had been running myself ragged trying to keep up my demanding schedule and pay off the debts that had been run up. I was not succeeding. How could I? It was an impossible task. My stress levels grew higher and higher, and finally, after years of trying to fight it, it began to affect my health.

In 1994, after talking it over with my mother, who agreed to help support me financially, I quit my job. With all the other pressure I was under, I was just finding it too difficult to perform. My car was repossessed because I could not make my payments. In most places in America, but especially in California, a car is more than just a possession. It's independence. Losing my own personal means of getting around and doing things for myself was hugely demoralising. On top of that, all my debts went into collections. It meant that debt collectors would keep my file on their records for at least seven years. They also reported the defaults with credit report agencies, so my credit rating was completely ruined.

It was back to the temp agency for me, but now I had to borrow my mother's car to go to my various jobs. My stress levels increased again, and I could feel myself starting to get sick. I couldn't put my finger on it, but I knew something inside me just wasn't right. I also felt that if I didn't get out of California for a while, and get away from the insanity my life had become, I was really going to lose it. In my stressed-out state, I hit upon an idea that sounds strange even to me now: Kenny and I would go to Hawaii on a vacation.

My mother paid for our trip. I think she understood what I was trying to do, and she understood that questioning me at this point wouldn't yield any clear answers. So she sent us to Maui, even paying for a rental car.

It was an odd trip. It didn't feel at all like a vacation. I just drove around the island with Kenny sleeping in the child seat on the passenger side. He was about fifteen months old at this time. Looking at all the other happy people on vacation just made me feel overwhelmingly lonely, and the fact that I had no idea what I was going to do with myself when I got back to California meant my stress level remained high. Meanwhile, I could feel myself getting sicker and sicker.

I was completely lost and alone in Hawaii. I had gone there because I had always seen it advertised as a kind of paradise where one could forget one's troubles. In my weakened state, I began to believe that going there would somehow change me into the kind of person who could relax and deal with life's problems more easily. One might say I had become so depressed that I was actually a little delusional. This was only to be expected, of course. One cannot carry such a heavy burden day after day, year after year, and not expect there to be eventual consequences. Sooner or later, something had to give.

One day, out of desperation, I picked up the Maui phone book and went through all the names until I found one that looked Vietnamese. When I dialled the number, a young man answered. I explained to him that I was a Vietnamese woman alone on her own in Maui with a little boy. I was looking for a Vietnamese family to connect with in order to feel a little more at home. Could he help?

Thankfully, he was only too glad to oblige. He, his girlfriend and his family were very kind to me, first taking me sightseeing, then to dinner at a Vietnamese restaurant. I can only imagine now what they must have thought of me, a random stranger appearing out of nowhere, asking for their hospitality. My sadness and purposelessness must have been obvious to them. No doubt they felt sorry for me and wanted to do all they could to help. I remember that family today with warmth and gratitude.

Over the next few days, I took Kenny on a snorkelling trip and then to a traditional luau. The snorkelling was amazing. I had never done this before, and I was astonished to see so many hundreds of colourful fish. Kenny, of course, was too little to snorkel, but he stayed on the boat and threw pieces of bread to the fish. The luau was also a great experience. The Hawaiian people take an entire pig and wrap it in banana leaves. Then they dig a big hole, make a fire in it and bury the pig in the hot coals. It cooks inside the leaves, which help prevent it from burning, and when it's done they remove it and have a feast. At sunset, some dancers performed a hula, a traditional hip-twisting dance, on the beach. Set against the backdrop of the sun going down over the Pacific, it was breathtakingly beautiful.

Then we went on to Honolulu. There, it was too hot even to go on the beach, so we just went shopping, spending money I didn't have, while my feelings of depression and anxiety only grew.

After a week, we went back to California. Of course, nothing had been resolved. I still had this terrible, empty feeling inside, yet I tried to act as if I was having a good time both in Hawaii and at home, like I was confident and full of sunshine.

But something had finally changed for me, though perhaps even I didn't know it at the time. I had never actually travelled for pleasure before – at least, not that far. I realised that I liked it very much, but, more than that, I also enjoyed letting people know about where I had been and what I had done there. It was more than just showing pictures and telling stories. It was adventuring in the true sense of the word. I did not know much about the art of travel writing, but a seed was planted in me on that trip that would blossom into something worthwhile some years later, when I became a website owner and entrepreneur.

Before that could happen, however, I still had several issues to deal with. Soon after our return, my emotional distress began to manifest itself in real, physical ways. I began having terrible digestive problems. Nothing I ate would stay in me. I had diarrhoea constantly and was in the bathroom all day long, every day. Nobody knew what was wrong with me, but, eventually, I was diagnosed with a hyper-digestive disorder and was told I would need two weeks of radiotherapy in order to solve the problem. I would be unable to care for Kenny during this time, and asking Mother to look after him was out of the question. Our emotional connection had not improved any over the years and, as she was working, it was impossible for her to take care of him.

I had no choice but to take Kenny to Paris, to stay with N's family. It was an awful trip, partly because I was so sick and partly because it was an eerie repetition of what had happened with Sonny. I couldn't believe I was in the same situation all over again, feeling forced to give up my child. This time, however, the circumstances were different, and in part I blamed N. If he had been a better husband and father, if he had not left us to go to France, then my life would not have been in the shambles that it was.

Sure, OK, maybe it was my fault for marrying him in the first place. And maybe he had hoped for more out of the marriage than I had been prepared to give. But this recognition of the mistakes I had made could not change the situation as it was at the time.

The pain of living was something I had been ready to give up at the age of eleven, when Mother and I jumped off the fishing boat and into the sea. I had been surprised when that wave washed me up on shore, and even more surprised at how happy I was to find myself still breathing. But still, I remembered feeling a slight twinge of disappointment that I was not going to get away with dying that easily.

Now, here I was, sixteen years later and not much better off. And there was no solution in sight. It might sound crazy, but when I thought back to the person I was in 1979, as Mother and I left the refugee camp in Malaysia, part of me looked at that destitute, homeless, speechless, scared little girl with envy. As much as we had suffered, at least at that point we still had a future to look forward to. How badly I wished now that I could turn back the clock and go back and do things differently! How much I wanted to hope again!

But I did not wallow in these thoughts for long. I was too sick. I dropped Kenny in Paris, watched with a mixture of joy and terrible sadness as Sonny played with him, then I said goodbye to my two baby boys and went back to California, alone.

The nature of my radiotherapy meant that I couldn't get too close to other people or I would risk contaminating them. I endured this isolation for two weeks. There were some unpleasant consequences to the treatment. My skin developed brown spots, and I felt very weak all the time. But eventually, it seemed that the cure was working. My digestion stabilised, and I no longer had to run to the bathroom constantly. I began to feel slightly human again.

With nothing else to do for the moment, and still feeling desperately alone, I began going to the same casino in Los Angeles that my mother frequented. There, I met S. He seemed rather taken with me, and my ego needed a boost, so we began seeing each other. He took me out to nice restaurants, and on weekends we went to karaoke clubs, where he sang me romantic love songs. S had a very good singing voice. No one had treated me this way before, and I loved it. I also loved the sex we had together – it was amazing. It went a little way towards filling the emptiness I felt inside my soul.

Soon after this affair began, however, I started receiving phone calls from someone who would hang up after hearing me say 'Hello?' I grew suspicious. When it happened over and over, I finally lost patience. I demanded, 'Why don't you speak, instead of hanging up like a coward?' After a long pause, a woman on the other end identified herself as S's wife. I was speechless with horror. I had become the other woman!

I'd had no idea he was married. How could I have? He spent all his time partying and singing songs, behaving as if he was 100 per cent eligible. He had lied and misrepresented himself. I was infuriated and heartbroken. Was there no man on earth who was trustworthy, who would keep his word once it was given?

S's wife and I agreed to meet and go to the casino where he spent all his time. We walked in together. If I hadn't been so upset, I might have found the expression on his face to be funny. As it was, the whole thing really bothered me, as I had liked S a lot. I didn't say a word to him. I just turned around and left him to deal with his wife.

If life had seemed empty before, now it seemed as big as outer space itself. I was floating, lost, adrift, with nothing – not even my children, or my so-called husband – to anchor me.

A month or so after this, a friend of mine invited me on a three-day cruise to Mexico with her and her boyfriend. It sounded like fun and a good way to relieve the tedium. Plus, who knew? I might meet someone interesting.

But this trip, too, became strange. One morning, after I had crawled in bed next to her and we lay there talking, her boyfriend came in and began teasing both of us. She responded by caressing his penis until it grew hard – right in front of me. Maybe they were into having a threesome with me, but, in Vietnam, sex is a very private matter, and I had never lost that sense of modesty. Embarrassed, I got up, ran out of the room and went to sit in the bar. There I fell into a conversation with a couple of young girls. We exchanged phone numbers because they said they would like to visit California sometime. I didn't know if I would ever see them again, but it felt good just to talk. I was reaching out to anyone I could, trying to make some kind of a connection – any kind.

Once I got home again, I had yet another affair, this time with a young man who really was very immature and nothing more than a user of women. I went out with him because I was lonely – that was it. He was one of those people who can sense loneliness in others and use it to his advantage. His idea of fun was to play pool and drink beer all the time, so that was what we did. But I got sick of that very quickly, and I let him go without much regret.

This kind of behaviour went on for the better part of a year. I did not have the means to support either of my children at this point, so I did not return to France to retrieve Kenny when I had fully recovered from my mysterious ailment and the radiotherapy. Sonny, by this time, was already lost to me. I knew that N's family would never let him go, and, as much as it hurt me to admit it, I knew both my sons were better off in Paris anyway. I tried not to think about it, but this situation hammered away at my self-esteem day after day. What kind of person can't support her own children? I asked myself. Ironically, once again, this was the kind of situation in which it would have been more advantageous to live in a developing country, where one can get by on very little. Sure, we would have been living in a tiny shack, with not much food, unsafe water, no medical care. But we would have been together. It's a question that I often pose to myself these days. Who is better off: the family that lives together in poverty, or the family that lives apart in comfort?

It's not such an easy question to answer, is it?

N came back to California on a business trip in 1996. He very quickly found out that I was seeing other men, and this must have rankled with his sense of masculine pride, because he began looking all over town for me. I knew he was searching for me, but I couldn't have cared less what he thought. I was sure that he would only be bothered because it made him look bad, and so I did my best to avoid him.

When N got back to France, he called me and presented me with an idea that had never crossed my mind: he wanted me to move to Paris. It was not right that our sons should be without their mother, he said, and the way I was acting was truly alarming him. Besides that, his brothers and sisters, who so far had been providing Sonny and Kenny with a lot of their care, were now old enough to move out on their own, and they were no longer willing to assume responsibility for the boys.

I told him I would think about it. I didn't care if I ever saw N again, but in fact I missed my sons so badly that it was like a huge weight around my neck. Once you have become a mother, there is a piece of your heart that can never be satisfied, except by seeing your children happy and healthy. The fact that my babies had been across the ocean and away from me all this time had been silently killing me.

In April of 1996, I decided to make the move. Really, there was never any question of me not going. I had nothing to keep me in California. I sold everything I could, put the rest in storage and said goodbye to Mother. She, too, was moving on – to Phoenix, Arizona, with her latest boyfriend. So things were about to change in a big way for both of us. This time, however, we were going our separate ways. I felt little sadness at this. I was grateful for the support she had given me in recent years, but we were still at loggerheads with each other all the time, arguing, fighting and trying to impose our will on each other. It would perhaps be for the best if we didn't see each other for a while.

Now, ten years later, it's easy for me to look back and grow philosophical about the journey I was on – not my literal journey to France but the journey of my life. But at the time, I had no thoughts other than to get out of California. Once, America had represented hope and promise for me, but my life there hadn't lived up to my dreams.

I had already come so far in my life that it was difficult for me to comprehend the enormity of the distance I had travelled – not just physically, of course, but culturally and emotionally as well. Sometimes, I felt like my soul was still trying to catch up with my body. I had started out in life as a simple Vietnamese village girl. Now, here I was, an American citizen going to live in Paris. Maybe things would be better for me in France.

Once more, I crossed Thuy Tinh's realm – this time miles above it, in the comfort of an aeroplane. When I disembarked in Paris, it was to begin the third chapter of my life on three continents.

Part 3

France, 1996–2006

13

Paris

I was twenty-nine years old the first time I ever saw snow fall.

It was the winter of 1996. At the time, N, Kenny and I were living in a tiny apartment in the 11th arrondissement of Paris. This area is famous for Père Lachaise Cemetery, an old burial ground in which many legendary figures – including Honoré de Balzac, Edith Piaf and Jim Morrison – are interred. We had a little window that overlooked the cemetery, and I was astounded to look out one day and see that the ranks of palatial crypts and ornate stone markers for which this cemetery is famed were blanketed under inches of white. Nothing could have prepared me for the sheer beauty of such a sight. I was reminded, too, of my dear Aunt Tuyet, whose name had meant snow. Tuyet would have loved to see such a thing. It would have taken her breath away as surely as it did mine.

The year 1996 was one of record cold in Paris, with temperatures hovering well below the freezing mark for months. Having spent all my life in the tropics or southern California, such cold was a new sensation for me, and I didn't like it one bit. The skies, too, were always grey that winter, and the steely clouds above seemed to match the grey stone walls of the ancient city, so that everywhere you looked, everything was the same drab shade of nothingness. In California, the sun had shone nearly every day without fail. Here, it seemed that weeks could go by before it dared peek out from behind the clouds. This kind of weather struck me as ominous. I missed the bright skies and warmth I had left behind.

But I was back with my boys, and so I was happy. Although Kenny was with me, Sonny was still living with his grandparents. There had been no discussion about this and no argument. I knew better than to try. It pained me to know that I had essentially given up my son before I really even knew how to be a mother. But given the depths of my post-natal depression, I knew also that the first few years of Sonny's life had been immeasurably better this way. And a mother's first concern is always that her baby is safe – even if she herself is the one he needs to be kept safe from. This may be difficult to understand for someone who has never experienced what I went through, but motherhood is a complex thing. At least N's parents lived only one Metro stop away from us, so I did not have far to go to see my boy. And they did not try to prevent me from seeing him. I could come and visit as often as I pleased.

Finally, the pieces of my heart that had been missing for so long had clicked back into place. A certain restlessness had been calmed in me. I was a mother again.

Moving to France was a big step, and nothing about it was easy. Before I'd even arrived, I had a reputation as a difficult and temperamental person, someone who was not easily dealt with. N's family, therefore, treated me with a certain amount of aloofness and disdain. I was also the woman who couldn't care for her own children; I was seen as selfish and wilful. I had always been viewed that way, throughout my whole life. These were not pleasant labels to bear, but I have to admit that in some respects I had earned them. Yet, in a way, they were also a mark of pride. I was not one to lie down and get stomped on by men, the way the vast majority of Vietnamese women were. If I felt a wrong was being done to me, I spoke up. I had lived long enough in the States, and had moved there at a young enough age, for the culture there to fundamentally change me. It was no longer possible to say of me that I was just a simple Vietnamese village girl steeped in tradition. Those were my origins, yes, but I was very American in many other ways – and those were ways I did not intend to change.

I had given up a certain amount of freedom to be with my family again. For one thing, as an American citizen with no legal status in France, I was unable to work. That meant long, monotonous days of staying home and doing nothing but cooking, cleaning and caring for Kenny. For another, I found myself – for the second time in my life – living in a country where the language and customs were utterly foreign to me. Languages had never been my strong suit to begin with, and French made my head hurt in the same way English once had years earlier. It had taken me almost a decade to achieve a high degree of fluency in English. I was not looking forward to the prospect of being wordless for the same amount of time in French. Of course, I would study and apply myself. But it would still take me a long time, and, in the meantime, there were many other difficult issues to deal with as well.

I felt just the same as I had when I arrived in the US eighteen years earlier, except now I was pushing thirty, married with two children – and not much else to show for my time in America. I had not achieved the 'American dream', whatever that was. I was neither a millionaire nor the wife of one. I had been very sick for a long time and depressed for years before that. One might say that I had actually moved a few steps backwards in the days since we had left the refugee camp in Malaysia. Things had not worked out the way I thought they would. I knew that I bore some of the responsibility for this, because of some of the decisions I had made – for example, getting married too young and for the wrong reasons. But I also knew that I was struggling against obstacles that most other people never have to deal with. And I was proud of myself in a way that I could not explain to anybody.

I was proud of myself simply for being alive.

Naturally, just because I was back with N did not mean we had suddenly rekindled our love for each other. We had never been in love in the first place. We were not even particularly glad to see each other again. I was still very angry with him. I laid down the ground rules for him when I first arrived – you do your thing, I'll do mine, and let's try to meet in the middle as far as the children are concerned – to which he seemed more than agreeable.

But one area where I was not willing to compromise was finances. The difficulties I had encountered with the credit-card companies back in the US had nearly ruined me – physically, financially and emotionally, and I would be damned if I'd let it happen again. I could put up with the fact that our new apartment was tiny – I knew Paris was an expensive city and rents were outrageously high. I could put up with the fact that he worked from noon to midnight every day, once again leaving me to manage every other aspect of our household, including all of the child rearing. What I could not, and would not, put up with was uncertainty about money. He promised he would be up front about his expenses, and he would tell me how much he made. I was not optimistic, but I had no choice but to take him at his word. I had no one else to rely on now – not even my mother.

If it wasn't for my beloved children, I often thought, I would have no one and nothing in Paris – in fact, no one in the whole world – to call my own.

Despite their initial coldness towards me, my in-laws tried to be helpful as I adjusted to my new surroundings. They came over and helped paper our apartment. They also assisted us in buying furniture, a washing machine and a refrigerator. These were no small purchases, and I was grateful for them. I probably did not show my gratitude in as purely Vietnamese a manner as they would have liked – meaning total humility and subservience – but that was not my way, and they would have to learn to accept that. Besides, I knew they weren't actually buying these things for me but for their son and grandson.

Our kitchen was so small that only one person could fit in it at a time, so we hired a handyman to come by and remodel it to create a little more space. He did his work and left a bill for 4,000 francs – at the time, the equivalent of several hundred dollars. N told me that he had paid the man what he was owed, so I didn't worry about it. Imagine my surprise then when, a month later, there came a banging at the door – and there was the handyman, babbling angrily in French. I couldn't understand anything he was saying, so I called my in-laws, had him speak to them and then translate for me. The handyman claimed he had never been paid!

My shock quickly turned to rage. I didn't doubt for a moment that the handyman was telling the truth. N hadn't changed at all. He was still deceitful to the point of being cowardly. What I had done to end up with such a despicable husband was beyond me. I had to pay the man out of our household budget, which meant I was left with practically nothing for bills or food. I began to wonder if I was even capable of living in the same country as the man I was married to. Every time he got involved in my life, I became miserable – and he didn't seem to care that he was always hurting the people who depended on him and whom he should have loved the most.

When I challenged him about the situation he explained that he had tried to contact the man several times about the bill but that he had never picked up the phone. But by this time, I was too angry to listen to his excuses. There are no words to describe the way I was feeling – rage, hatred and loathing do not even begin to cover it. Yet there was nothing I could do about it. I had to swallow my feelings and carry on. Once again, I began to slide into depression.

Things proceeded in this manner for a long time. Weeks quickly became months, and I made little progress in adjusting to life in Paris. I had never really spent any time in a major city before – Los Angeles is a very spread-out kind of place, and one never has the feeling there, as one does in Paris, New York or London, that one is 'downtown'. Paris intimidated me. People walked too fast, street signs were incomprehensible, shop staff were rude, and the transit system scared the daylights out of me. It was easier just to stay inside all day with my baby, like an ostrich with its head in the sand.

* * *

In August, as I began to get seriously depressed again, I decided that I would once again try a little bit of travel as a way to distract myself and shake myself out of the doldrums. It hadn't really worked in Hawaii, but something had been awakened in me on that trip. I was beginning to discover an inquisitive part of me that had never been fed before. I wanted to see more of the world. I didn't need to fly thousands of miles – the entire nation of France was new for me. I was insecure about the way people looked at me on the streets of Paris – I felt that there was some prejudice against me for being Asian and for the way I dressed, which was not *à la mode* – but I was tired of sitting in my apartment all day. So, I decided to break out of my shell and take Kenny to Lourdes.

Lourdes is a Catholic shrine, sacred to the Virgin Mary. It was a place that I had long been interested in. In 1858, a young girl named Bernadette was out gathering wood when she heard a gust of wind, looked up and saw a lady dressed in a white robe with a blue belt. She spoke to Bernadette briefly and told her they would meet again, which they did, on a regular basis, and eventually the woman said she was the Virgin Mary, the mother of Jesus. Of course, when Bernadette began to tell people what she was seeing, few believed her. She was threatened with arrest by the Church and was the subject of much mockery at first. But then people started to believe, and things reached the tipping point.

The Virgin appeared to Bernadette many times, eventually directing her to drink from a spring that at that time was nothing more than a puddle of muddy water. She also told her to eat the bitter herbs that grew around it. At first, everyone thought she was mad, but then it was noticed that the water had healing qualities. A girl who had a dislocated shoulder dipped her arm in the water and was cured. The apparition told Bernadette to tell the priests to build a chapel there, which they did. Today, there is a magnificent shrine on this site that has been visited by millions of the faithful, many of whom claim miraculous cures from the waters. Indeed, there are thousands of pairs of abandoned crutches and wheelchairs left behind as a testament to the power of faith to heal.

Although my family in Vietnam was officially Catholic, I had never been religious. Yet I felt drawn to this spot for some reason, perhaps because I was in so much pain myself. Surely, I thought, if the Virgin can cure physical ills, she can help with emotional ones as well.

Also, there was something about the story of Bernadette that appealed to me. We had a few things in common, she and I. Like me, she was full of determination, even when she was the only one who believed in herself. I admired her greatly for this. Bernadette seemed strongly attuned to an inner voice that helped to direct her on her life path. In other words, she did not just *see* the Virgin, she also had the courage to follow her words, even when faced with ridicule and punishment by the ignorant people around her. I liked that part of the story best of all. It seemed to me that life would be so much easier if only I could get in touch with that kind of inner strength. I knew it was there – I wouldn't have been alive if it wasn't. I just had to find it again.

I won't make any dramatic claims of immediate successes after my visit to Lourdes, nor did I see any visions of the Virgin Mary myself. But something did change for me on that trip. The world began to open up for me as it never had before. We had taken the TGV, the special high-velocity train that crosses France, to get to the shrine. I realised that this train, easily accessible from our apartment in Paris, would allow me to see much of the country cheaply and quickly. I could zip halfway across France in the morning, spend the afternoon in some interesting locale, and be back in Paris in time for a late dinner. Moreover, since the train was very popular with international travellers, many of the staff on board spoke English. The language problem was therefore removed. The seed that had been planted in me in Hawaii began to grow again. I still had no concrete ideas about what this all meant. But I knew I loved to travel. Maybe it was because I had been forced to move around a lot in my life and now I was going places because I chose to. Somehow, I thought, maybe I would be able to turn this into something.

Yet my own personal vision was still some years away from becoming a reality. I had not yet heard much of this strange new thing called the Internet; I was unfamiliar with computers, as were most people. Yet change was coming, and coming soon, for everyone.

But all things, great and small, are accomplished one step at a time.

In September of that year, I went to the US Embassy in Paris to get my passport renewed. While I was waiting, I picked up a publication called *France–USA Contact* (*FUSAC*). It was in English, and it was written for the American community living in Paris. I was overjoyed to discover it. Why, I wondered, had it taken me so long to realise there were other people like me in the city? My fear of the unknown had kept me isolated and alone for nearly a year. No more, I vowed. Now I began to see that I was no longer just a victim of bad luck and unfortunate circumstances. I began to understand, little by little, that if I expected anything to change, it was completely up to me to make it happen. There was no way I was going to rot in that tiny apartment, always broke, afraid to go out. I was now thirty years old, I had not yet even entered the prime of my life, and it was time for me to wake up.

As simple as it sounds, another thing galvanised me into action: my new passport. Looking at it casually, I realised that it was a brief but telling account of my life so far: born in Vietnam, naturalised in California, now a resident of Paris, France. I had lived in three countries on three continents, each of them so vastly different from the other that they might as well have been three different solar systems. Mine was an unusual experience, sometimes for good reasons and sometimes for bad. But I began to understand and appreciate something about myself: my story was my own, and it made me who I was. It was time for me to stop complaining about the way I was treated by others. Time to stop being passive, accepting whatever life handed me, and time to start making things happen for myself.

I took the copy of *FUSAC* home with me and read it again and again. There was a programme, I learned, called 'Bloom Where You're Planted', designed to help new arrivals learn to fit in better in Paris and to discover all that the city had to offer. The very name of the group encouraged me. It reminded me that we can't always choose where we end up in life, but we can always choose how we deal with it – and we can do so with style and grace.

The 'Bloom Where You're Planted' programme was due to begin the next month, October. I registered immediately and then could hardly wait. The group met on Tuesdays. That first Tuesday also happened to be Kenny's very first day of school. He was too young to stay at school for lunch, so he was to come home at noon. That conflicted directly with my meeting. I foresaw this and mentioned it to N, thinking he could help me by giving Kenny lunch that day himself. I should have known better than to even ask. Of course he couldn't do it, he replied. Whatever I had planned was nowhere near as important as whatever it was he was doing.

I could see that I was going to have to fight N every inch of the way for my freedom. Well, I had survived much worse than him – the Viet Cong, the shipwreck, the refugee camp, being a runaway. Compared to these obstacles, he was no more than a minor stumbling block. Too bad he couldn't realise that both our lives would have been so much more pleasant if only he would learn how to treat me like a person instead of a slave with no will of her own. Oh, well – I wasn't going to waste any more time worrying about him. I missed that first Tuesday meeting. But for the next meeting, I made other arrangements for Kenny, leaving him with his aunt and Sonny, and then I was free to go.

That day was rainy, but the weather did nothing to dampen my spirits. I waited in the downpour to catch the No. 69 bus near the Metro station Chemin Vert and rode it for nearly an hour, all the way through downtown Paris, to the place where the meeting was being held. I could hardly believe my eyes at the landmarks I saw along the way. The bus passed the Place de Voltaire, the Bastille, Le Marais, L'Hotel de Ville, the Palais Royal, the Louvre, the famous Musée d'Orsay, and the Invalides. I also saw the Eiffel Tower up close for the first time, as well as the Arc de Triomphe. I had been in the City of Light for almost a year, and this was the first time I was seeing any of these places. I realised that I could, any time I wanted, take different bus lines to see all the parts of Paris. It wasn't nearly as terrifying as I had thought it would be. And the cost of the journey in each direction was ridiculously low: less than the equivalent of one euro, or about one US dollar. Even if I had never made it to the meeting, just the trip alone would have been worth it.

But I did make it to the meeting. The group comprised mostly American women, all of whom were white, obviously better off than I was financially and at least ten years older than me. I was glad to hear English being spoken again, but I felt out of place among these wealthy society women. They did not treat me badly; it was just my natural shyness and insecurity coming to the fore. I was not well dressed, and I have always looked much younger than I really am. At one point, one woman actually asked if I was there with my mother.

Yet I was still very glad I went. For one thing, the programme's presenter did a great job of explaining the Metro system. It was such a simple thing for Parisians, but if you didn't understand it, you were helpless. Just this little bit of information alone was enough to have a big impact on me.

I went home and thought about things. Inside me, everything was changing, but change is a slow process and cannot be rushed. I was no longer content to spend every day in the apartment, but I was still not secure enough to take Kenny with me on the Metro. I had nightmares about losing him, or having him taken away by a stranger, or about both of us getting lost and never finding our way home again, since I would be unable to explain myself to a policeman. For most people, these fears might seem over the top, but after being uprooted so many times and losing all that was near and dear to me at such a young age, these were not just irrational worries. I still did not know it consciously, but, after two decades, I was still feeling the emotional fallout that comes from being a child in wartime and a refugee. My stubborn, independent streak was not quite ready to admit what is now painfully obvious – that I had been badly damaged as a child, and as a result I would always be different from all the other people around me. I would not be able to change until I admitted this to myself. I don't mean that I needed to indulge in self-pity but that I had to put it all behind me and move on.

It sounds like an easy thing to do. Yet part of me was resisting this very strongly. In order for me to make progress, I would have to forget that all those terrible things had ever happened. I would have to reach a stage where it was as if they had never taken place. But how could I forget such traumatic events? It was not possible for me to just wipe them from my memory. They were a big part of my identity. Instead, I would have to let go of their significance. Since they formed such a large part of how I saw myself, this would be a very difficult thing to do. It would take a long time. But I knew for the first time that I was strong enough to do it.

There was another war raging inside me now. It was between a scared little girl on the one hand and a grown woman on the other. The woman was offering her hand to the girl, saying, 'It's all right, come with me, there's nothing to be afraid of.' But the little girl was too frightened even to hear what the woman was saying. She would rather have stayed in her scary world of exploding bombs, flying bullets and sinking ships, surrounded by the shadows of fear and loss, than move forward into an unknown future. Why was there even a question as to which was the better path? Standing back and looking at it from the outside in, it seems so obvious what I should have done years ago. I should have forgotten my past and embraced the future. So why didn't I? I don't have the answer to this, but I do know that all of us have these two parts inside us: the adult and the child.

You can usually tell within moments of meeting someone which one is winning the fight inside them.

Also, as I said, change – deep, meaningful change – is always slow. And I must be compassionate with myself. Looking back over the first forty years of my life, I can see that I wasn't moving as slowly as I thought. After all, I had started well back from where most people begin. Few Westerners had had to cope with my kind of life; it wasn't even possible for me to explain my history in a way they would understand.

But, finally, in my thirtieth year, things began to change.

In November, I joined the International Women's Club. This was a new organisation that had been created only that year by a British woman and two French women. These three had been living abroad for most of their lives and had decided to form a club for foreign women who lived in Paris, regardless of their nationalities. At the time, there were only sixty members. Most of the women were in their forties and fifties, so, once more, I was one of the youngest. But I was a little stronger and more secure now, so this did not bother me as much.

I attended that month's meeting at the Novotel Hotel, which overlooked the Seine, near La Défense. This is where many of Paris's high-rise office buildings are situated. The name originates from a monument, La Défense de Paris, that was erected in 1883 to commemorate the war of 1870. The view of the city from the top floor was spectacular. We all spent some time getting acquainted with each other, and this time I convinced myself to be more outgoing and make more of an effort – and not to be mistaken for anyone's daughter!

Most of the women had husbands with important jobs for large multinational corporations, and a few even had high posts in the government, but I vowed that I would not be intimidated and would chat with them as equals – and I did. Later, we went downstairs to have a three-course lunch with wine. It was a most elegant affair, and I enjoyed it hugely. I began to realise that these women weren't just wealthy. They were – most of them, anyway – very interesting and intelligent people. Best of all, the woman who had volunteered to work as the club's membership director was Vietnamese, although since she was much more conservative than I, we had little in common. Before that meeting was over, I had volunteered to work as a hostess for the club, and I had made some new friends.

Just like that, I belonged. The little girl had taken the woman's hand and was beginning to follow her into the unknown.

For me, the key was in volunteering. No longer was I going to wait for people to be nice to me. Instead, I would make the first move. It was a decision that very quickly began to reap rewards – not in any financial sense, since that is contrary to the spirit of volunteering, but instead in a much more valuable way. For the first time in my life, I began to meet new people and make friends with them on a regular basis.

I liked it. I was hooked.

Next, I joined a group called WOAC, the Women of the American Church. Although it was a religious organisation, they did not insist on anyone attending church services. The emphasis instead was on getting together once a month and listening to various speakers. I quickly made myself available to coordinate these meetings. This involved a lot of work – finding an available apartment, establishing the agenda, locating interesting presenters and setting up the actual meeting. But I loved every minute of it, and I made a great many new friends through this organisation as well.

The third organisation I became involved with was WICE – the Women's Institute of Continuing Education. This was a group that was started several years earlier with the intention of allowing foreign women living in France to take further education credits but had since evolved to admit men, too. Through this group as well, I made many new friends – including some who were shortly to become important to me in my next venture, the founding of *Paris Woman Journal*.

Over the next few years, I continued to get involved on many levels with all these groups and more. In the meantime, life went on more or less the same at home. My boys grew and thrived. N and I remained married but distant. We took some interesting trips – to England, back home to California and to other places in Europe, North Africa and Asia. My mother came to visit, and I was astounded to see how many young men turned their heads to stare at her on the street. I had never known before that young Frenchmen were so interested in older women. Mother hadn't changed a bit – she revelled in the attention, even though she pretended not to notice.

I still struggled with depression and loneliness, especially at night. I guessed that my mother might also suffer from these feelings, even though she would never admit it. We were different, however, in that I didn't feel that I needed a man to take care of me, and I have since shown that I am more than capable of looking after myself. But still, I battled against the fear and insecurity that was implanted so deeply within me.

Sometimes, the ghosts of my past came back to haunt me. I thought of my little sister, Hanh, and wondered what she would be like now if she had survived. I thought of my father, and how even though when he was alive he had nothing to give us, his service to his country had allowed me to come to America and begin a new life. I thought of all those poor people on our boat who had died in the struggle to escape the Communists. I looked back at my years in California and thought of all the things that I wished had happened differently.

But any change that is worthwhile comes slowly. If it happened all at once, it wouldn't be worth anything. My bad times slowly began to recede. I cannot say they disappeared, but they did stop ruling my life. Little by little, I was laying the foundation for what was going to come next.

Juliet Lac was about to take the next step on her long journey.

14

The Founding of pariswoman.com

ate one night in April of 1998, as I lay awake in bed, I had an idea. It came to me as a result of my recent experiences as a volunteer with all the different organisations I was now involved with. I had learned that I was not the only non-Parisian woman living in Paris – even though at times it certainly felt like I was. Clearly, there were other women who were feeling homesick and out of place. Also, I had learned the importance of getting out and meeting people, regardless of how uncomfortable this was at first. And, of course, it is especially important that women have the opportunity to socialise with other women. So, I thought, why not do something different to help bring women together, and allow them to just sit and talk, while at the same time providing them with a way to learn more about Paris – showing them in the process not just how to get by but to thrive?

And, of course, there would be something in it for me personally. I would get to make new friends in the process. I would be branching out. The little girl was making rapid strides in the direction of the woman. In fact, there was no stopping her now.

But how was I going to do it? Paris did not need another women's social organisation, not even for English speakers. There were already plenty of groups filling that gap. While I felt they were an excellent way to meet people, I also thought that there was still something missing from them – pure information. I was full of questions about Paris, but I couldn't very well bombard our speakers, or even the other members of the organisations, with constant enquiries about how to find this restaurant or that museum, or how to get the bus to some particular part of the city. There had to be a reference guide of some sort – a place where English-speaking women could go to find interesting places that would appeal to their sense of style, taste and culture. And I wanted to share other kinds of information, too – unexpected titbits that would pleasantly surprise them and feed the soul. I wanted to know about more than just what places in the city were trendy or chic. I also wanted to find places that were somehow meaningful, that would really allow people to feel connected to the city and to have a sense that they belonged.

I had been thinking these things for a long time, but I had not yet articulated them to myself. Then, that night, everything crystallised, and the idea came to me in a flash: I would create a journal.

It was a daunting prospect. I was still intimidated by the prospect of writing and communicating in English, but I had learned by now not to let my fears constrain my actions. I would get help and thereby make it a collaborative effort.

I could hardly sleep that night because I was so excited. The next morning, as soon as it was a decent hour, I picked up the phone and called several women I knew from my volunteer work. I asked each of them if they would be interested in helping me and if they would lend their creativity and expertise to the project. All of them eagerly said yes, and we scheduled our first meeting at a friend's home.

Everyone was very excited. First, we needed a name. After some discussion, we came up with something simple: *Paris Woman Journal*. Then, we brainstormed about what kinds of articles it should contain. There should be something for every type of person, we decided, and it should also address all those areas that we ourselves had had questions about when we first moved to the city. The big issues were public transportation, schools, child care, grocery shopping – all those things that we take for granted when we are at home but which are often incredibly difficult when dealing with a foreign language.

In addition, we would write about culture – how to take advantage of the incredible wealth of art, music, history and architecture that Paris had to offer. I got excited all over again listening to everyone's ideas, and I got a big charge out of realising that my original plan had excited them, too. It was a completely new experience for me to connect with people in this way. Also, I found myself in a totally new role: project leader. Already, I was making rapid progress on my new path.

By this time, I had managed to teach myself a good deal about how to use a computer. In fact, it's fair to say that for my first few years in Paris, my computer was my only real friend. Once again, my old flair for self-teaching had come back, and I learned a tremendous amount about a wide variety of programmes. I did so well at this that I was able to hire myself out as a computer consultant to various friends who were not yet as knowledgeable as I was and who needed help getting their own home systems set up. With Microsoft's FrontPage software, I learned how to build and launch websites. The very first site I ever built was called *SDImaging*, which provided online printing services for digital photos. It sounds complicated – and it was. But I was proud of this first effort. Interestingly enough, soon after this, N – who by now had started his own photo-finishing company – suddenly came up with the brilliant idea of adding a digital component to his services.

I began designing the layout of *Paris Woman Journal* using Adobe PageMaker. I spent hours and hours playing around with different concepts, feeling energised in a way that I never had before. A friend from WICE, Cliff Lee, did some very fashionable drawings for the cover. After endless amounts of reformatting, plus the time spent in gathering the articles everyone had promised to write, the first issue was ready for distribution.

It was twenty pages long. There were some basic flaws – I had omitted to put the date anywhere, for example. But it was done, and it looked pretty good. Once again, I was very proud of myself.

My plan was to distribute *Paris Woman Journal* as a free paper, or ask for a donation of the equivalent of two euros, since I was not yet allowed to earn money legally in France. I could afford to print only a few dozen copies, so I took them to the places where English-speaking women were most likely to see them – the American church, the Embassy and a few other places in the city. In the meantime, we began work on the second issue.

But already there were problems. None of the women who were working on the project with me were professional writers. They did not quite grasp the importance of deadlines, and the work they did turn in was sometimes not up to the standard I had hoped for. Usually, it was left to me to polish the articles up – which was a challenge – and I was in charge of the layout as well. I spent many, many long hours putting everything together. There were a few days when Kenny didn't even get to go to school, because I was too tired to get him ready in time. That wasn't too much of a problem, though, as it was still only pre-school, and he wasn't missing any vital information.

Perhaps the most challenging aspect of the whole venture was that I had to pay for the printing of it out of my own very limited personal budget. N was still very careful when it came to letting me have any money – not just for myself but also for the household. By this time he had given me an ATM card, but there was a limit to how much I could withdraw every week. As if I were a child, he had me on a strict allowance, even though the only things I wanted money for were to run our home and to take care of his own son. So, instead, I used the money I made from computer consulting to fund the printing of the journal. I never regretted this. It was my idea, after all. And the pleasure I derived from seeing my own creation in its physical form was unparalleled.

But eventually, the problems I faced in printing the journal became insurmountable. The women who worked with me had their hearts in the right places, but there was an imbalance in terms of who was putting in the most work. I was doing nearly everything, and paying for everything, too, even though among all of us I was least able to afford it. The articles they turned in were often only half-finished or not in a format that worked for a magazine. Most of the time, they were late. A few were simply never delivered. It was too much for me to be editor, proofreader, layout designer and distributor. Eventually, I threw up my hands and said that I was done. After just four issues, *Paris Woman Journal* was being put to sleep.

But it was immediately to be reincarnated in a new form – an online version. I had realised some time ago that the Internet was the place where things were going to be happening from now on. One of the reasons I hadn't already switched over to an online version was that connection fees in France were outrageously expensive at the time. As in most places in those early days, one still had to pay by the minute, rather than a flat monthly rate. But now that the print version was done with, I could focus all my energy on something that was actually easier to produce. With the web, I didn't have to pay for every copy I wanted to print, and I didn't have to travel around the city, lugging boxes of heavy paper from place to place. Whenever the site needed to be updated, I could do it from home, without having to redo the entire layout. All I had to do was publicise the domain name – www.pariswoman.com. And the best part was that I could now attract contributors without having to go through the frustration of putting together more meetings. These contributors could also be based anywhere – not just in Paris but anywhere in the world. As long as the articles followed the same theme – enhancing the quality of life for English-speaking women in Paris – they would be considered.

Suddenly, I was very glad I'd been born in time to live in the age of the Internet. I began to sense the possibilities that awaited me, and I lost no time in going after them.

I spent hours and hours late into the night putting together the website. I publicised it by posting announcements at all the regular haunts for English speakers, and I slipped it into conversation whenever I could. In the first month the site was up, I had about 100 visitors. I was elated – this was already more people than had ever read the print version!

I soon realised that the site had some fundamental design flaws, and I took advantage of the communicative power of the Internet to post a query on a website for designers about how to make my site look better. This is just another reason why the Internet is so amazing – it can allow experts from anywhere in the world to share information with neophytes like me instantly. I loved it. It was like walking into a room of total strangers and asking their opinion on something but without having to worry about whether or not I would be accepted by them. I did not have to deal with shyness or uncertainty about language, either. These designers looked at my site design and tore it to shreds, but in a constructive way. They also gave me some invaluable tips on design that I would be able to carry into future projects.

My main concern was that pariswoman.com be easily accessible for women who might not be very Internet-savvy. I wanted it to be simple to navigate. Of course, as in so many things in life, making something look simple is tremendously complicated. But eventually I finished my redesign, and then the site was really something to be proud of.

Gradually, the site began to generate its own buzz. More and more ideas began to occur to me about how to make it even better. I could use the site for a web log, or 'blog', where I could post a daily column about whatever I wanted. Whenever something I thought my readers would be interested in was about to happen – a new restaurant opening or a new museum exhibit – I could add that to the site right away. Soon, people began approaching me with ideas for columns and articles. I also connected with American writers living in Paris who wanted some exposure. For the last hundred years and more, Paris has drawn thousands of literary expatriates with its mystique and its history. Now, instead of writing in some little garret and hoping against hope that they would be published, like Hemingway or Fitzgerald, hopefuls could instantly see their journalistic work online.

And I could branch out into ever more directions. Today, pariswoman.com offers information about culture, news, opinion, travel, networking – any subject that could possibly be of interest to English-speaking women in Paris. And the number of interested readers has grown exponentially – from 100 in that first month, to hundreds every day. To generate revenue, the site also features adverts.

In short, it was a success.

Every time I logged onto my site now, I felt a sense of pride. I saw all the activities it covered, and I got a thrill all over again when I thought of the many different kinds of people from all walks of life who could find something to interest them on the site. In a way, I had been able to realise a dream that I still had trouble with in the physical world – feeling connected to people, lots of people. Perhaps it will seem ironic to some that this happened online rather than in the flesh. But I firmly believed that technology is not just a meaningless frill or a luxury that interferes with our lives and wastes time, like television. Ideally, it should enhance our lives and bring us together. This is precisely what the Internet does. I would advise all women, regardless of who they are, to learn how to use the Internet as soon as possible, even if only for simple things such as sending and receiving email and being able to look things up on a search engine.

I was often made to feel different and not good enough when I was a child and a young adult, but racial boundaries and cultural borders fall away online. And the notion that I could ever have done something like pariswoman.com in Vietnam is laughable. Even if I had survived life under the Communists, Vietnam is in some ways still a Third World country, and most people do not have access to computers. It is likely that I would still be living in some tiny little house somewhere in Ben Tre, an ignorant housewife, never having seen anything of the world and the wonders it contains.

It's interesting to note that harsh Communist regimes, such as those in China and North Korea, feel the need to regulate the kinds of things their citizens can access online – if they are allowed online at all – whereas in free societies, they can read and publish whatever they want. In the twenty-first century, although it seems incredible, many millions of people are still living under harsh authoritarian rule. The Communists still don't seem to understand that dissent is a good thing; that it can help make a society stronger and more innovative – not less. Will they ever see this? Probably not. The Communist ideology in itself is flawed, because it requires people to surrender their free will and behave like robots. You can say what you like about the United States. It is not a perfect place by any means. Like any society, it has its problems. But one thing you can be sure of is that, as a citizen or resident, you will have the freedom to access whatever information you want. People may be subject to a certain amount of 'capitalist propaganda', for example, in the form of commercials and advertising that urge us on in the blind consumption of goods. There is much about America that still surprises me, and sometimes even embarrasses me. And sometimes the government is less than forthcoming with its people about certain events that might make it look bad. But, by and large, the truth is there to be discovered.

With the collapse of the Soviet Union – an event that brought joy to my heart, as it did to hundreds of millions of others around the world – we have seen that Communism is unsustainable. I hope that the Internet continues to be one factor that makes this obvious to everyone in the world, regardless of who they are. Eventually, people will come together to throw off the shackles of oppression. They will remember that there is strength in numbers. Technology can help them do this.

I believe this with all my heart.

Over the next few years, I made constant efforts to keep the site up to date, adding new features whenever possible. But as technology moved on, it eventually became outdated, and I had to face a new challenge: learning a new way of coding that would allow more people to access the site. This was a very daunting task, and at first I decided it was beyond me. So I concentrated on achieving another dream.

One of my greatest goals in life had always been to get a university degree, but I left America without completing my studies. Because I wanted to set an example for my sons, I was highly motivated to find a school where I could enrol and finish what I had begun. It wasn't important to me that I go to a prestigious place such as Harvard or Princeton. All I wanted was my degree so that I could take advantage of whatever new opportunities that would bring me in my life.

The easiest way for me to do this was to enrol at the Open University in the UK for online courses, so I signed up for a BA course in Business and a BSc course in Technology. I started my first course in 2001, took a final exam in Paris after ten long months of writing essays, and then learned, to my great joy, that I had passed my first course. After that, I took two full-time courses each year. It was tough to study on my own, but it was worth it.

The success that I enjoyed with my studies made me feel empowered, and my thoughts turned once more to improving the website. This time I was determined to overcome the technical difficulties I had encountered, and with a lot of help from a site on CSS coding run by a man called Joe Gillespie, I was eventually able to successfully redesign the site, making it available to many more people.

For me, this was proof I could achieve anything I set my mind to, and I was extremely grateful for all the help I had received along the way. It also encouraged me in my studies, and in October 2005, I finally obtained my BA in Business Studies, and a year later, in October 2006, I earned my BSc in Technology, thus realising two major ambitions within a year of each other.

15

Friends Around the World

The website opened the world up to me, and led me to take a greater interest in everything that was going on, both near to home in Paris and further afield. In 2003, the spectre of war appeared on the horizon again, this time in the Gulf, as tensions mounted about Iraq and its supposed Weapons of Mass Destruction. There was a lot of hostility between France and the US, due to disagreements over the best way to deal with the situation, and I received a lot of messages enquiring about what it was like to be an American living in Paris at this time.

'How are we expatriates holding up over here?'

'Are the French mistreating us, now that they officially hate us?'

'What about all the French Muslims, do they give us dirty looks and hurl anti-American slogans at us?'

In other words, people were asking if we were OK.

I had given a lot of thought to the subject, as I had just returned from my first visit to Tunisia, a Muslim country, during the Christmas holidays. I travelled there with my son, Kenny, and the experience had such a profound effect on me that I now felt obliged to share my own unique perspective on Americans, Muslims and the French.

It was hard, at first, to begin writing about my thoughts on the Tunisian people. As I've explained, this was my first visit to a Muslim nation, and before we went I did not know what to expect. I wasn't sure how we would be received, and at first I was a bit unnerved, as people seemed to stare at us a lot. But I soon realised this was nothing but natural human curiosity, and the warmth and smiles of the people there remain with me still. To say I was deeply touched by the people is an understatement, as during our trip we were welcomed without hesitation. People wanted to know where we came from, and far from being put off by us being Americans, they asked for more details.

'Which state . . . Texas?' they enthusiastically asked.

When we said that we were in fact from California, they gave us even bigger, lovelier smiles and said, 'California is great!'

There was no hostility towards us because we were Americans, and it reminded me that the most important thing human beings can do when they encounter new people is to communicate and accept each other's differences. The most poignant reminder of this came from watching my son, Kenny, play with children, both in Tunisia and in other countries we have visited on our travels. Children just inherently know one thing that we Westernised adults often forget: how to interact with others honestly and without expectations.

In some ways, I felt more welcome and accepted in Tunisia than on any of my regular visits back to my own adopted country of the United States. Landing there after escaping the war in my native country of Vietnam, I lost my identity at a very young age. I risked my life in the rough ocean to find freedom and the chance for a better life and thankfully I found those opportunities in America. But I did not always feel welcome, and the sense of having given up my birthplace and become a nomad of sorts has never completely faded. It was reinforced each time I returned home to Orange Country, when fellow Americans in grocery stores or malls asked, 'Where are you from?' When I said I was an American, too, I sometimes felt that people doubted me or were suspicious.

This used to bother me, but not any more, as my experience of living in Paris made me recognise how incredibly young a country America truly is.

And so when I was asked, 'How do the French see us?' I answered that the French see America as I do: as a young country that does not want to learn from the mistakes of our older cousins, but instead insists that our cousins adopt our modern ideals. They see America as a young society that thinks older societies are outdated and in need of change; as a young society that views poverty as a sign of weakness and political mismanagement. They see America as a young nation that thinks because it is faster and stronger it is always right and should always be in charge.

And in many ways we Americans *are* faster and stronger and do make good leaders; but, like a bull-headed teenager, we are not always right and not always properly informed. As we mature, it is my hope that we Americans will come to understand what history has to teach and that we will use those lessons wisely. Perhaps then we will stop associating one man's political actions with the religious beliefs of an entire population. I also hope that, as we mature, America will come to understand that while poorer nations may lack our obvious material wealth, internally they can prove far richer because they've found fulfilment in their traditional values and beliefs. Perhaps then we'll cease resenting other nations for depending on us as much as we regularly insist they do, or cease expecting everyone to speak English whenever we travel and to serve us McDonald's and Coke alongside their indigenous couscous and maize. I guess what I was really trying to convey to anyone accessing the website at that time was that the French and the Muslim people as a whole do not hate Americans.

On the website I wrote:

> Paris is not burning and we are not paying for the sins of our fathers. But if pressed, any Frenchman will tell you that what they do dislike is the arrogance and intolerance we regularly display towards those who disagree with us. And when looked at from that point of view, I have to agree.

The website has also allowed me to meet and make friends with many women I would not otherwise have come into contact with.

In February 2002, for example, I met Vernita Irvin through pariswoman.com. Vernita had moved to Paris from Los Angeles with her three cats. She works as a freelance writer and had written several screenplays for Hollywood films. By chance, she discovered pariswoman.com when she was browsing on the Internet for information about Paris and non-profit American organisations. She immediately sent me an email enquiring if she could participate and write for the website.

While in Paris, Vernita managed to find a part-time job at an airport shuttle company so she could pay her rent and cover her other daily expenses. I routinely invited her to lunch at my place, and sometimes she would bring friends who were visiting at the time. She took creative writing courses in London and was working on a mystery novel. Vernita was a great friend who helped me and inspired me to write.

In early 2004, an editor friend invited me to a girls' night party at her flat in Levallois-Perret. It was an event that highlighted how powerful the Internet can be as a networking tool. One of the other women who was going to attend was called Carolyn. Carolyn and I had met a little over a year earlier through pariswoman. com. She'd written to me and introduced her Virtual Assistance business in Paris. After a few emails, she invited me to lunch, and we met at La Défense for a hearty meal. What began as a business meeting quickly turned into a long discussion about our lives in Paris. We had so many things in common, especially being entrepreneurs, and I talked to her at length about the website, particularly its purpose and goals.

When Carolyn asked what the site needed, I immediately said, 'Writers. I need good, mature writers who have lived in Paris, either in their dreams or for real.' Carolyn looked at me and said, 'Well, I may just have someone for you.'

About a week later, I received an email from Carolyn inviting me to lunch with Priscilla. 'Wow,' was my response. 'You are really quick!'

As a result of that meeting, Priscilla became the editor of

our new feature 'Paris: Through My Eyes'. Through Priscilla, I then met Tamiko, who told me that she met Priscilla through pariswoman.com! After reading an article Priscilla wrote on Internet publishing, Tamiko contacted her. So now at the girls' night party, I knew three people, and it was a pleasure to introduce Tamiko to Carolyn.

In July 2004, I received an email from a writer friend in Australia announcing that she would be coming to Paris the following month. So I arranged a luncheon meeting with two other friends at a brasserie in Montmartre. We had a good lunch and spent nearly three hours talking and reminding ourselves of our first meeting that had taken place a year and a half earlier at Bercy Village in the 12th arrondissement. After lunch, we visited the plaza at Sacré Coeur, where artists exhibit their wares while musicians and performers entertain the crowds. The small streets were packed with tourists, and the atmosphere was lively and colourful. We took several photos before heading back down the hill and ending our adventure at the Anvers Metro station, where, after a few well-placed kisses, I was on my way home. I smiled throughout the whole journey as I thought about how we had all met each other quite by chance . . . on the Internet.

Another significant friendship I made on the Internet is with Marina, a Russian whom I met several years ago through the website. She contacted me after living in Paris for six months and asked if we could meet for lunch. (Lunch is an important meeting time in Paris, in case you hadn't noticed!) We met at a lovely restaurant in the Marais, where I learned that Marina had recently married her French husband after meeting him in Moscow. She was introduced to him by a contact at work who asked Marina to show the visiting Frenchman around the city. It was '*coup de foudre*' Marina says, love at first sight. Soon afterwards, she moved to Paris. 'No regrets, we are happy!' she assured me at the time, and we have since become close friends. Our families have often eaten dinner together, and we enjoy each other's company tremendously.

The Internet is a valuable network where people can meet and forge genuine relationships, if they do so with the right intentions. At pariswoman.com, we stress this in our forums section, where we urge people to make contact with one another and see what happens. Traffic in the forum is slow. Our readers are primarily women with very busy lives. We all have careers, children and husbands, and that doesn't leave much time for emailing. But if the connection is made, it can lead to some very satisfying results.

Take my friend Margaret, for instance. I also met Margaret through the website. She'd done an extensive search on the Internet for websites about Paris, and after prolonged correspondence, we became good friends. Margaret is a writer and in 2005 she published a book about her French language lessons in Paris. She writes extensively about the phenomenon of Internet relationships.

Most of the vibrant, exciting people who have contacted me through the website are professional women who wish to enlarge their circle in Paris, and I can certainly understand this desire. As women, we often need another purpose, something that is outside of our duties as wives, mothers, businesswomen and carers. We crave the opportunity to share our stories and relax with people who don't have to be like us, but who understand us.

In short, women need girlfriends.

During my first two years in Paris, I was deeply depressed. I had no friends, no close relatives, no family and no way to communicate. All I had was my son and his love, and although he remains the well of all my hopes and motivation, as a result of starting the website I have built up a group of strong women whom I count as my close friends, and I now also have the friendship, warmth and support of readers and friends from all over the world. To me, this is both priceless and essential.

16

Return to Vietnam

I was eleven years old when I left Vietnam in 1978. I left to find freedom and a better life in America, and when I left California in 1996, it was to live with my family in Paris. Throughout this time, I'd thought I would never want to return to Vietnam until the country was free from Communism. Somehow, however, my mindset changed, and I think this was as a result of my travels with my youngest son to other parts of the world, including Tunisia, Turkey and many countries in Europe. In every country that I have lived in or visited, I have always had a feeling of being a tourist, a foreigner. There was often a sense that I was only expected to spend lots of money and then leave. I can still see the look in the eyes of the locals in some countries, as if they were saying, 'Welcome to my country, now go home.'

Everywhere Kenny and I went in Europe or America we were a minority. I had long been used to getting stared at by people who weren't accustomed to Asian faces. Even though Asians in a broad sense can be seen everywhere in the world these days, there is a difference between, for example, Vietnamese, Japanese, Taiwanese, Korean and Chinese people that may not be visible to Europeans but which is obvious enough to us. I did not feel at home among a group of people simply because they had Asian features, any more than a white person from Alabama would necessarily feel at home among a group of Romanians. To put it simply, there was only one place in the world I could go and not be considered a tourist or a foreigner, and that place was Vietnam.

Living in France, which was the capitalist oppressor of Vietnam for so many years, had given me many opportunities to learn about my birth country, especially as the French are very connected to the Vietnamese. The former French President Jacques Chirac's adopted daughter is Vietnamese, and one of France's most famous singers, Johnny Hallyday, and his young wife recently adopted a baby girl from Hanoi. They apparently also have plans to adopt a Vietnamese brother for their new daughter. Hallyday's wife was quoted in a major French daily newspaper as saying: 'I did not carry her in my womb, but I will carry her in my heart.' I was deeply touched by this, and I also felt in many ways that France was trying to come to terms with its legacy of exploitation in Vietnam.

In early 2005, therefore, I decided to take my son home with me to Vietnam. And once I had made this decision, I felt an unexpected surge of excitement, as if I was going on my greatest adventure yet. I called my mother to tell her what I was planning, and her reaction was first one of surprise, then interest. She wanted to go home, too. She often thought of Vietnam, of course. When we left, she was already in her mid-thirties. She had many more memories of the place than I did, and for her, the adjustment to life in America may in many ways have been more difficult than my own, because she was older, though of course I had not thought about this at the time. She would never think of any place other than Vietnam as home, she said, and, yes, of course she would come.

Mother was still living in Arizona, so she flew to Paris to join up with Kenny and me, and in late February, we made the trip back to our home country with a group of French tourists. Ironically, although one of the reasons I wanted to go home was because I was tired of feeling like a visitor, it was still easier to get around the country as part of a tour group than to travel independently, particularly as I would be travelling with my son.

When we arrived at the airport in the city that I still thought of as Saigon, I explained to Kenny how it had been re-christened Ho

Chi Minh City in 1976, after the war ended, and then, of course, I had to explain who Ho Chi Minh was and how his struggle for independence had inspired me, even though in many ways it had ended up being a disaster for the South and had hurt the North a great deal as well.

There are some disadvantages to travelling in a large group, and we had to wait five hours for everyone to get through passport control. Then we had to put our heavy baggage through a second X-ray machine again at customs. It took a while to locate our tour leader, Hung, outside the airport, and there were so many people in the group that it was quite difficult to gather everyone together. But finally he took us to our hotel. We had two hours to take a shower and rest before we reassembled in the hotel lobby for a quick tour of the city.

My first impression of Ho Chi Minh City when travelling in from the airport had been negative. I did not like what I saw. I did not like the crowds. I did not like the motorcycles. In fact, I disliked nearly everything about the modern Saigon. The noise was unbelievable. So was the dust. On every street, it seemed that people were eating – at little tables, as they stood on a corner, as they walked along. When they were done, they tossed whatever they hadn't finished into the street and then washed their bowl in open communal containers of water that had been set out for that purpose – there was no hot water, naturally, and no soap.

My own personal standards of cleanliness had evolved immeasurably in the last twenty-seven years – I shudder now to think of the piles of trash and swarms of flies that I once took for granted – and I didn't think I would be able to eat a bite anywhere we went. When I reflected once again on the fact that this was my birth country, I felt a sense of disappointment.

But this feeling vanished as we began our tour. Slowly, I remembered what the pulse of life had felt like in Saigon, and I started to absorb it once more. It seemed to me that the people were both tight-knit and open. Everywhere on the roads, people stopped their motorcycles in the middle of the street to have a leisurely chat, forcing everyone else to go around them. There was never a moment of quiet or of boredom.

Our tour began with a visit to Notre Dame Cathedral. Next, we crossed the road to the post office built by Gustave Eiffel in 1891, eight years before he completed the Eiffel Tower in Paris. Already I was beginning to feel a deep connection between my birth home and my current one. Next, we took the bus to the covered market, called Ben Thanh. Here, you could find everything and anything your heart desired. The market was so crowded that we could hardly squeeze in amongst the buyers and sellers. Everywhere you looked, people were bargaining over handmade goods and produce. It was exhilarating, and I revelled in the fact that, for the first time in a long time, everyone looked like me. This might sound strange, perhaps even slightly racist. But it wasn't that at all. It was just that I was beginning to feel that I had come home.

The pace the next day was non-stop as, after breakfast, we visited the Presidential Palace; then another church, Cha Tam; the Chinese quarter Cho Lon; then the Giac Lam and Thien Hau pagodas. We then paused for lunch, but before long we were back on our feet visiting the Museum of History; Vinh Nghiem, the city's largest Buddhist pagoda, and another, Ngoc Hoang. As Buddhism is the main religion in Vietnam, there were many pagodas to see. Although more than eighty per cent of Vietnamese people today say that they have no official religion, Buddhism was the main religion before Communism, and it continues to be a huge influence today. Spirituality is fundamental to many human beings, and that doesn't change simply because people are living under Communist rule. It just means that they learn how to keep their mouths shut and not say what they are really thinking.

The third day saw us up at dawn, heading for Tien Giang, a province seventy-two km south of Saigon. The capital city of the province, My Tho is situated in the middle of a huge network of canals in the delta of the Mekong River, which connects to the China Sea.

To the French people on the tour, the visit to My Tho was just another outing. But it was here in this precise spot, twenty-seven years earlier, that Mother and I had last set foot on Vietnamese soil and surrendered ourselves to Thuy Tinh's will. Together with 350 other people, I'd spent seven days and eight nights on a tiny fishing boat in the middle of the ocean. Nearly 200 of those people were drowned when the boat sank while in sight of the Malaysian shore. It was hard to believe that Mother and I had survived the journey.

I had been curious as to how I would feel at this moment, for I had never had the opportunity to revisit a place that held such importance in my own life. Since I had last set foot here, I had been a refugee for nearly three decades, always moving, never feeling settled anywhere, never feeling at home. I don't mean the casual sense of getting used to a place but rather the deep sense of belonging that comes from being in the land of one's ancestors, a feeling in one's very bones.

Mother, Kenny and I went to the banks of the river at the very point where we had embarked on the fishing boat nearly thirty years before. There were several of the same kinds of boats on the river at that moment, and I was amazed at how small they were.

'How many people did we have on our boat again?' I asked my mother.

She did not answer me at first, because she was feeling some very strong emotions. But when she could speak again, she said, 'Three hundred fifty.'

'How did you fit so many on one little boat?' Kenny asked.

I looked down at him. I hoped so strongly that he would never, ever have to undergo what I went through at his young age. To this day, I cannot explain why I survived that journey while so many others died.

'We almost didn't,' I said. 'And a lot of people died.'

'How long were you on the boat?'

'Seven days, eight nights,' Mother and I both replied automatically.

Kenny was impressed, though I could tell he had no sense of what had really happened. I wasn't going to try and labour the point. I was glad he didn't know. I don't believe children have an obligation to understand their parents' suffering. Their duty is simply to live their own life. And for those who made the kind of journey that my mother and I did, they will hopefully have the supreme satisfaction of knowing that they sacrificed everything so that their own kids could be brought up in freedom and safety. That is enough. Yes, OK, it gets a little frustrating when my son's biggest concern is getting new batteries for his GameBoy. At his age, I was more worried about death by dehydration or starvation. But I don't begrudge him the fact that his life is better than mine, or that he will have so many more opportunities than I had. Once we become parents, our focus shifts from taking care of ourselves to taking care of the next generation.

The next day we boarded the aeroplane to Da Nang, which is the third-largest city in Vietnam and one of its main ports. In Da Nang, we visited Cham Museum, which was created in 1916 and which houses a fine collection of Champa art from the fourth to the tenth centuries. From there, we continued on to Hoi An by bus. Hoi An is an ancient city with many historical sites. The hotel where we stayed was fabulous, and I regret that we only got to stay one night. We left early the next morning, on our way to the city of Hue, about 110 km further north. During the four-hour journey, we crossed the famous mountain road called Deo Hai Van, which overlooks the gorgeous Lang Co peninsula. The ancient city of Hue was once the capital city of Vietnamese royalty, and it is loved by many famous Vietnamese intellectuals and writers. In 1993, UNESCO declared it a World Heritage site, and as we visited the Imperial Citadel, I felt its rich history.

After visiting Hue, we flew up to Hanoi. Hanoi is now the capital city of the unified Vietnam, but from 1887 it was the capital of French Indochina, and there is a strong French influence in the architecture. My first impression was that the people there were not as friendly and open as the people we met in the South and Central Vietnam. I saw no smiling faces, and everyone appeared subdued as they went about their busy daily lives in the city. My mother, Kenny and I also attracted some strange looks, as we were the only Vietnamese travelling with a group of white foreigners. However, I was impressed by the charm of the city, its lakes, gardens and the famous red bridge at Hoan Kiem Lake. We took a ride on a xich-lo (cyclo, or tricycle) in the city centre, passing the Old Quarter of Hanoi with its small side streets filled with a variety of shops. This particular area is also called 'The Quarter of 36 Corporations' and as we passed streets like the 'Street of Silk' or the 'Street of Cotton and Fabric', I understood why. Shopping was the order of the day, and I found the silk shops were fabulous. Later, we dined at one of the best restaurants in the city.

Early the next morning, our bus headed to Ninh Binh, about 100 km south of Hanoi. Ninh Binh was the home of the ancient Dinh and Le dynasties. As part of the trip, our group boarded some long, narrow wooden boats for a two-and-a-half-hour trip along the river. Passing rice fields and mountains, we visited the caves of Tam Coc, Bich Dong and Dich Long, and three mountain pagodas. The boat ride was fantastic, especially when we had to go through the dark caves.

The next day, we headed out to Hoa Binh, about seventy km south-west of Hanoi. Here, we visited a tribal village and watched a special performance by the local young men and women, who wore different tribal costumes for each dance. It was a great show, and everyone really enjoyed the entertainment. After the performance, we were invited to taste the tribe's alcohol. It was stored in a tall jar and we drank it through bamboo pipes. The drink was a speciality of the region, and I felt touched by the warmth and hospitality of the people.

The two last days of our tour took us to Ha Long Bay, where our hotel room had a full view of the magnificent bay and its famous rock formations. On the night of our arrival, I bought an ao dai in one of the beautiful silk shops, and I wore it on board the boat while we went for a tour of Ha Long Bay the next day. It was then that I felt like a true Vietnamese girl.

In the afternoon, we headed back to Hanoi and prepared for our flight back to Paris the next day. As I thought back over our adventure, I felt strongly that it was the best trip of my life, and I planned to visit again in the future, but on my own next time, not on a tour or with my family, so that I can visit the places of my past, mainly the places where I was born and had lived during the war.

My trip back to the land of my birth made me realise that there is a place on earth where I belong, but it also made me realise how far I have come on this journey through life and helped me to look at my mother in a new light.

Back on that third day of our trip as we stood on the banks of the river at My Tho, I simply could not believe that we had crossed the ocean in such a tiny frail craft. And I was suffused with a powerful sense of two times coming together into one. For a moment, I could almost see the eleven-year-old me stepping fearfully onto the boat, right in front of me. How I wished then that we had the ability to part the veil that separates one time from another, that the grown me could somehow have reached out to my younger self and offered some kind of assurance. But all I could do from where I stood was to watch the whole journey unreel in my mind once again, scene by horrifying scene.

As I stood there breathing in the river-scented breeze, I wanted to point out the old fishing boats and tell the French people in the group about my journey, but my French was still not good enough to tell the whole story fluently. No doubt they wondered why I was crying. Mother and I didn't talk much, either. Then again, we didn't need to. It was really not until this moment that I realised just how truly brave my mother was. She had made the decision to yank us out of Third World poverty and ignorance and land us in a better life in America, thousand of miles away – and she had done it. It was simply amazing.

I felt deeply proud of my mother and what she did for us. I

was proud of myself for surviving this far. And, for the first time, I was proud of being Vietnamese. The Communists will be gone some day, maybe in my lifetime, maybe not. But it doesn't matter. What I've come to understand – what I sensed on that tour of my homeland – is that Vietnam can never be stamped out, no matter who invades us, no matter who tries to control our lives and our affairs. We survived the Chinese, we survived the French, we survived the Americans. We will survive the Communists, too.

That's what it's all about for us Vietnamese . . .

Survival.

And this is what it's about for me, too. Just as my mother always said, I am like water: mercurial, tempestuous and unpredictable. But I am like water in other ways, too. Drops of rain will wear away the hardest stone, given enough time – like the Vietnamese said, '*Nuoc chay da mon*': eventually, a tiny trickle will find its way through the biggest mountain. Sooner or later, water overcomes everything. It cannot be defeated. I am Juliet, made of water. I have survived war, abandonment, drowning, shipwreck and much else. Many times, Thuy Tinh has had me in his grasp, but each time I have eluded him. I am still here, and I will continue on, unceasing in my efforts to carve out a life for myself in this hard world. Water never gives up. By its very nature, it cannot.

And neither can I.

Epilogue

A New Beginning

On our return from Vietnam, in September 2005, my relationship with N finally broke down completely, and he moved out. At first, he sent money each month for child and spouse support, but in March 2006 that stopped. After that, he seemed to disappear, and we received no letters, no emails or phone calls.

In the summer of 2006, therefore, I applied for a French residency card that would allow me to live and work legally in France. The interview process and the wait following it lasted for almost two months, and then in late September the verdict came in – no. My request had been turned down, and, furthermore, I had to leave France within two weeks of receiving this notice. It was my official exit visa from the country!

I appealed against the decision and was given another three months, but it seemed the original decision was to stand, and my son and I only had enough time to pack our clothes and buy our airline tickets before we hopped on a plane the day after Christmas to return to Orange County, California. Before we left, I made arrangements with our wonderful French neighbour, Christine, for her to help me give away the furniture and empty out the place as needed.

So, more than ten years after I left, I am now back in the US, starting all over again. This time, I have been lucky to have the help of friends like Sara, who let us stay with her until I found a job, and my mother, who lent me a car. I have also remembered all the valuable lessons I have learnt so far and put them to use to build a new life for myself, having qualified as a life insurance specialist.

It's still not always clear where this journey through life is going to take me, but I know that I am better equipped than ever to deal with whatever comes my way.

Writing this book has long been a dream of mine. I've always felt that my story could be important for a lot of people, for a lot of different reasons. But I did not want to tell my story so that I could hold myself up as an example of anything. I do not consider myself to be a model person. I don't think I have the right to tell anyone how to live. Nor am I meant to be a spokesperson for Asian women in the West. I wanted to tell my story for no other reason than that I, Juliet, am still here, despite everything. I am not just alive – I am prospering, flourishing, growing. It is not only the soil of America that nurtures me, but also the earth itself, and her gift of life.

But I do ask my readers to remember a few things.

Remember that we all have our humanity in common – and that that is enough.

Remember that we must treat each other with respect.

Remember that we are not here to take, but to give.

And remember, above all else, the sacredness of life.